# PRAISE FOR
## THE JOY CHALLENGE

"When is the last time you really felt joy? In a world full of stress and conflict, true joy can feel always out of reach, and Randy offers a path to discovering the kind of deep joy that feels like a constant companion."

**–CANDACE CAMERON BURE, ACTRESS, PRODUCER, AND *NEW YORK TIMES* BESTSELLING AUTHOR**

"Randy is one of my golf homies. Every time I'm with him on the course he's filled with joy, even when I'm beating him. *The Joy Challenge* leads you to his source. You gotta check it out."

**–TOBY MAC, GRAMMY AWARD-WINNING SINGER AND SONGWRITER**

"A compelling book that will inspire readers on a twenty-five-day Joy Journey with practical tips. Frazee's book could not be timelier to a hurting world that needs more joy. Practicing joy is our brain's super-fuel— activating a combination of our feel-good neurotransmitters of dopamine, endorphins, and norepinephrine. Yet too often we fill our brain with the toxic fuel of negative input and feelings, taking in an estimated 9 to1 negative to positive inputs. Frazee's book provides a road map, rooted in faith, to overcome our brain's bias toward negativity to reframe our circumstances with intentional brain habits of joy. The Joy Challenge could be the best thing you do to become healthier with a more vibrant brain to thrive in whatever unpredictable circumstances life throws at you."

**–SANDRA BOND CHAPMAN, PHD, CHIEF DIRECTOR, CENTER FOR BRAINHEALTH, PROFESSOR, UNIVERSITY OF TEXAS AT DALLAS**

"Randy Frazee is a world-class communicator and thinker. This clear road map to managing our spiritual, relational, and emotional selves into the obvious resulting joy is amazing. A clear must-read."

**–DAVE RAMSEY, #1 BESTSELLING AUTHOR**

"Joy is our apologetic as those who follow Jesus, and not just joy, joy unspeakable! Randy shows us how to experience it in new ways."

—MARK BATTERSON, *NEW YORK TIMES* BESTSELLING AUTHOR, *THE CIRCLE MAKER*; LEAD PASTOR, NATIONAL COMMUNITY CHURCH

"Is it just me or does joy seem to be in short supply these days? Our circumstances, our worries, and our world can make us start to believe that life is made up of just occasional moments of joy surrounded by days, months, and years of sadness and discouragement. But God's Word provides a road map to experience not just a few joyful moments, but a joy-filled life! And Pastor Randy's deep knowledge and understanding of Scripture make him the perfect 'joy guide,' helping you and me discover the fullness of joy God is offering."

—MATTHEW WEST, AWARD-WINNING SINGER AND SONGWRITER

"I wrote a song a few years back called 'What Kind of Joy.' I was blown away by the level of joy Paul from the Bible experienced given all the hardships he faced, including prison. Randy digs deep into the life of Paul to answer my question. Good news, it is available to all of us!"

—STEVEN CURTIS CHAPMAN, GRAMMY AWARD-WINNING SINGER AND SONGWRITER

"*Do you want more joy in your life?* Who doesn't? We all do. And the good thing is, the God of Joy has more joy to give. In *The Joy Challenge*, fellow pastor and joyous dude Randy Frazee takes you on a twenty-five-day, twenty-principle journey toward a joy-overflowing life. Take the challenge and you will see."

—KYLE IDLEMAN, SENIOR PASTOR, SOUTHEAST CHRISTIAN CHURCH; BESTSELLING AUTHOR, *WHEN YOUR WAY ISN'T WORKING*

"Having spent most of my adult life in the Hollywood scene I can tell you what doesn't bring one joy. As a Christian, I have become utterly convinced that the secret to true joy is found in God's Word. Randy extracts inspired principles from the book of Philippians and makes them accessible to all of us. Take the challenge and find the deep peace and lasting happiness we all long for."

—CHERYL LADD RUSSELL, ACTRESS

"Depression and anxiety are the new global pandemic. People everywhere are struggling like I have never seen before. *The Joy Challenge* is not just a book but an effective road map rooted in Scripture and backed by current brain research to enable us to rise above what is holding us down and to experience the life God intended. If you need that . . . dive in!"

—ASHLEY WOOLDRIDGE, SENIOR PASTOR, CHRIST'S CHURCH OF THE VALLEY

"To shoot par in the game of life you got to have joy. In Randy's newest book, *The Joy Challenge*, he becomes your personal swing coach to get you there.

—JIMMY WALKER, SIX-TIME WINNER ON THE PGA AND WINNER OF THE 2016 PGA CHAMPIONSHIP

"Randy does a masterful job connecting ancient spiritual scripture of the Bible to what we know about the brain today. Take on the challenge, exercise your hippocampi, challenge your prefrontal cortices, tune your amygdalae, and watch your joy grow! Your brain will thank you."

—DR. FONDA CHAN, NEUROLOGIST

"*The Joy Challenge* by my friend Randy Frazee is a tour de force for those wanting to move past their circumstances that are filled with worry and chaos. Each page is a journey toward understanding joy not as a fleeting emotion but as a gift from God that emboldens our lives."

—DUDLEY RUTHERFORD, SENIOR PASTOR, SHEPHERD CHURCH

"The apostle Paul wrote the Joy Book in the Scriptures—the letter to the church in Philippi. Taking the lead from Paul, my friend Randy Frazee amplifies and applies the book of Philippians for our generation. He leads the way with joy and dares us to live the joyous life. Enjoy the book."

—RUSTY GEORGE, LEAD PASTOR OF CROSSROADS CHRISTIAN CHURCH; AUTHOR OF *FRIEND OF GOD*

"Randy Frazee has the heart of a shepherd, the mind of a scholar, and the intuition of a loving parent, as is evident in his new book. The chapters are filled with encouragement to help readers look past their worries and focus on the One who deeply loves them. Rush out and add this book to your library!"

—CALEB KALTENBACH, AUTHOR OF *MESSY GRACE* AND *MESSY TRUTH*

# THE JOY
# CHALLENGE

# THE JOY CHALLENGE

## DISCOVER THE ANCIENT SECRET TO EXPERIENCING WORRY-DEFEATING, CIRCUMSTANCE-DEFYING HAPPINESS

# RANDY FRAZEE

NELSON BOOKS

An Imprint of Thomas Nelson

Published in Nashville, Tennessee, by Nelson Books, an imprint of Thomas Nelson. Nelson Books and Thomas Nelson are registered trademarks of HarperCollins Christian Publishing, Inc.

Published in association with Don Gates of the literary agency The Gates Group - www.thegates-group.com.

Thomas Nelson titles may be purchased in bulk for educational, business, fundraising, or sales promotional use. For information, please email SpecialMarkets@ThomasNelson.com.

Any internet addresses, phone numbers, or company or product information printed in this book are offered as a resource and are not intended in any way to be or to imply an endorsement by Thomas Nelson, nor does Thomas Nelson vouch for the existence, content, or services of these sites, phone numbers, companies, or products beyond the life of this book.

ISBN 978-0-7180-8623-7 (audiobook)
ISBN 978-0-7180-8620-6 (ePub)
ISBN 978-0-7180-8616-9 (TP)

**Library of Congress Control Number on File**

*Printed in the United States of America*

24 25 26 27 28 LBC 5 4 3 2 1

*To Westside Family Church*
*I thank my God every time I remember you. In all my prayers
for all of you, I always pray with joy because of your partnership
in the gospel from the first day until now, being confident of
this, that he who began a good work in you will carry it on to
completion until the day of Christ Jesus. (Philippians 1:4–6)*

# CONTENTS

INTRODUCTION                                                XIII


## PART 1 JOY DESPITE YOUR CIRCUMSTANCES

PRINCIPLE #1   RECALL HAPPY MEMORIES                          9

PRINCIPLE #2   LEARN HOW TO LOVE                             17

PRINCIPLE #3   SEE THE GLASS AS HALF-FULL                    27

PRINCIPLE #4   EMBRACE YOUR NO-LOSE SITUATION               37

PRINCIPLE #5   TAKE THE HIGH ROAD WITHOUT FEAR              47


## PART 2 JOY DESPITE PEOPLE

PRINCIPLE #6   GET ON THE SAME PAGE WITH YOUR
               COMMUNITY                                     63

PRINCIPLE #7   ELEVATE OTHERS ABOVE YOURSELF                71

PRINCIPLE #8   STOP BEING A GRUMP                           81

PRINCIPLE #9   CELEBRATE OTHER PEOPLE'S SUCCESS             91

PRINCIPLE #10  DO RIGHT BY OTHER PEOPLE                    101


## PART 3 JOY DESPITE YOUR PAST

PRINCIPLE #11  STAY CLEAR OF LEGALISM                      117

PRINCIPLE #12  RECALCULATE WHAT REALLY MATTERS             127

# CONTENTS

PRINCIPLE #13  PUT THE PAST BEHIND YOU  137

PRINCIPLE #14  FOCUS ON THE FUTURE  147

PRINCIPLE #15  SURROUND YOURSELF WITH

THE RIGHT PEOPLE  155

## PART 4 JOY THAT DEFEATS WORRY

PRINCIPLE #16  SEEK RECONCILIATION IN

YOUR RELATIONSHIPS  171

PRINCIPLE #17  GIVE WHAT TROUBLES YOU TO GOD  181

PRINCIPLE #18  REHEARSE YOUR BLESSINGS DAILY  191

PRINCIPLE #19  ACCEPT THAT MORE MONEY AND

STUFF ISN'T THE ANSWER  201

PRINCIPLE #20  LET PEOPLE HELP YOU  209

CONCLUSION: WRAPPING UP THE CHALLENGE  219

ACKNOWLEDGMENTS  223

NOTES  227

ABOUT THE AUTHOR  241

# INTRODUCTION

**W**hy do so many people struggle to grab hold of and hang on to joy and happiness? If you are one of them, trust me, you are not alone. Interestingly, the Declaration of Independence of the United States of America offers us this awesome promise: "We hold these truths to be self-evident, that all men are created equal, that they are endowed by their Creator with certain unalienable Rights, that among these are Life, Liberty and the pursuit of Happiness."[1] Our founding fathers explicitly stated that it is God who grants this right equally to all people. That includes you and me. So, what in the world are we missing? Could the one who allocated this birthright to us in the first place know something we don't about joy? Are you interested in taking a journey with me to find out?

Six decades in and counting, I am confident in my conclusion that just about everybody on the planet is searching for the holy grail of joy and happiness. The fact that you are holding this book in your hands would lead the average person to assume that you have outfitted yourself in your khaki safari garb and are on the hunt along with the rest of us. Welcome, sojourner, to the worthy search for this seemingly universal longing.

But I don't want to make any assumptions. If the search for happiness really is a worldwide pursuit, it would be reasonable to Google something like "The World Happiness Report" to find out if anyone has figured out the secret. Which I did. What did I find? Surprisingly, I found that Nordic countries such as Finland, Denmark, Iceland, Sweden, and Norway are where the happiest people on the planet live.[2] I say "surprisingly" because the word *Nordic* means "North" and refers to countries in places that get super cold. Places that regularly reach sub-freezing temperatures cannot be the epicenter of joy and happiness—at least that's how I feel about it! But the global research, year after year, keeps putting Nordic countries at the top of the 150 countries studied.

So, trusting that research, we try to find the secret to their success. When Denmark was at number one, we were told it boiled down to their lifestyle practice called *hygge*. Hygge (pronounced "hoo-gah") means cozy and comfortable and is essentially accomplished by sitting around a fireplace with family and friends. That sounds compelling, given the fast-paced, go-go-go culture in which most of us live. So, as you might imagine, all kinds of books, articles, and even household products were sold by the millions (seriously, you can buy hygge candles and hygge games). However, as of the writing of this book, Denmark has declined in the happiness rankings for several years, slipping to number three in the world, and hygge products have been relegated to the clearance corner. (I still think hygge is a good idea.)

Lately, Finland has ranked number one in happiness. Their secret sauce is not as redeemable, in my estimation. They call it *kalsarikannit,* which translates as "pants drunk." This is the practice of binge drinking home alone in your underwear. One Finnish person wrote in response, "If this is a secret to happy life, let's keep it that way: a secret."[3] I agree. Staying drunk all the time does not seem like a particularly effective way to hold on to happiness. So, how have they held the number-one spot for four years in row?

In the article "The Grim Secret of Nordic Happiness," Finnish writer Jukka Savolainen uncovered the basis for the results of the *World Happiness Report*, a survey of people all over the world that asks them to "imagine a ladder with steps numbered from zero to 10. The top rung (10) represents the best possible life for you, while the bottom rung (zero) represents the worst. The survey participants are then instructed to report the number that corresponds to the rung on which they are currently standing . . . you are deemed happy if your actual life circumstances approximate your highest expectations."[4] In other words, if the differential between the rung you are standing on and the rung that represents your highest expectations is small, then you are declared to be happier than if the differential between where you stand and where your highest expectations are is larger.

**NORDIC PEOPLE**

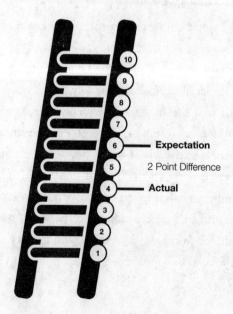

XV

Could there be something more at play here in the degree of happiness we think Nordic people possess? Let's look at something called the law of Jante. This is a code of conduct that encourages a collective unity while discouraging individualism. It says things like, "You shall not believe you are as much as us."[5] It comes from a satirical novel written in 1933 by Danish-Norwegian author Aksel Sandemose. It was originally intended to shed light on common attitudes in small Nordic villages but, like any good satire, it had an element of truth, and the law of Jante has now become widely accepted as part of the Nordic mentality.[6] Unity over individualism is a good thing for sure, but it also tends to lower a person's aspirations for the best possible life. So, the Nordic person's expectations can be super low, and the differential between their ideal, or best possible life, and where they currently place themselves is quite close. Maybe this explains how Nordic countries continue to rank among the happiest in the world. Mr. Savolainen brought his short article on Nordic happiness to a close by writing, "If that's happiness, count me out." I agree. I don't think this is the secret sauce of joy and happiness.

Neither do I think that places like the United States, which currently ranks at number sixteen, hold the key. We have crazy-high expectations of our best life in areas like wealth, fame, and power. We believe our children are the best, the prettiest, the smartest, and the most special people in the whole world. So, we tell them they can be anything they set their minds to. We may not suffer from extreme self-deprecation and thus have low expectations, but the gap between our current status and our expectations is often huge, resulting in colossal levels of disappointment, depression, and anxiety. That also can't possibly be the road to happiness.

## UNITED STATES PEOPLE

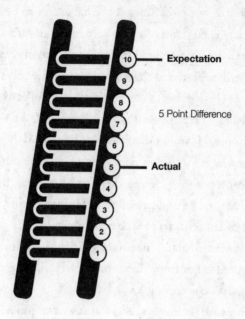

What the Nordics and the Americans share is the importance of our circumstances. Nordics lower their expectations so they can confuse their current state of melancholy as happiness; Americans raise their expectations to crazy levels and then spend their lives chasing the elusive "carrot on a stick." I have an alternative for you to consider. It's not my alternative but that of an ancient guy named Paul who wrote thirteen books of the New Testament. Of his thirteen books, inspired by the breath of the Spirit of God, Paul wrote one that turned out to be a treatise on joy. My interest is piqued. How about you?

Here's the kicker: The number one book on joy in the Bible was written by a guy in prison! You heard that right—prison. Paul taught us that joy is not dependent on our circumstances but is available to us in full despite our circumstances. We don't need to lower our expectations to increase the appearance of joy or work tirelessly to reach and sustain our ideal circumstances. As it turns out, we can experience true joy regardless of our circumstances. That seems to be a bit far-fetched at first glance, but I am ready for something different. Neither the Nordic nor American plan hold much promise in my estimation.

The book we'll be studying together as we pursue this third way is Philippians. It is clustered with three other books collectively called "the Prison Epistles," because Paul wrote them while he was under house arrest in Rome. He wasn't there because he did anything wrong; he was there because he wouldn't back down on living out his faith (which was his source of joy). He was there, as we will see, by the sovereign plan of God, and he understood that. He was writing this short letter composed of four chapters to the believers in the city of Philippi in the country of Macedonia. A man named Epaphroditus carried the letter eight hundred miles from Rome back to Philippi to give these folks the true scoop on accessing joy.

Paul used the word *joy* in its various forms sixteen times in this letter. The word he chose to express our English idea for joy in the Greek is *chara* (pronounced "khar-ah"). People who have *chara* possess an inner sense of contentment ("it is well with my soul, in spite of what is going on outside") and purpose in their life ("I know why I am here and what I am to do"). I don't know about you, but that is precisely what I want.

The problem for most of us is we allow joy robbers to come in and steal that sweet sense of inner contentment and purpose. Who or what are these bandits? Paul addressed four of them:

1. **CIRCUMSTANCES:** This is when our current circumstances stink or our preferred circumstances change.
2. **PEOPLE:** This is when other people enter into our space and mess with us. They disappoint us, attack us, say awful things to us, lie about us or to us, undermine us, or betray us. They throw us off our game.

3. **PAST:** This is when we can't get beyond the trauma of our past, either something we have done or something that was done to us. We're stuck and can't move forward.

4. **WORRY:** This is when we are riddled with worry and anxiety. In some cases, we know why we are so uptight; in other cases, we have no idea where it is coming from or how to dig ourselves out of the hole.

Paul didn't tell us how we can avoid these joy robbers—it is not possible. Paul faced each one of these robbers in the most intense way and yet ended up writing the treatise on joy. How? He took hold of joy for himself despite these four hoodlums. Through his teachings, we can learn how to have this same brand of joy despite these thieves' presence in our lives.

In this book, we'll address the four joy bandits, and in the section on each bandit, I'll share five principles for increasing our joy. That's a total of twenty principles. About half of the principles are explicit; that is, Paul laid out the axiom in plain sight and told us to put it into practice. The other half of the principles are implicit, meaning the principles are implied by the way Paul lived his personal life, particularly from prison. We are invited to mimic his behavior.

Before we get started, though, let me give you a clue to the secret of Paul's success. It comes down to your mindset. While Paul used the word *joy* sixteen times in Philippians, he also used the word *mind* sixteen times. There is a definite cause-and-effect relationship between the two. How you think and what you think about will drive your joy quotient. Your attitude, perspectives, and beliefs will govern where you end up on any given day. As the late Dr. Warren Wiersbe wrote, "Outlook determines outcome."[7]

What we have come to discover about our brains and our minds over these past five to ten years has turned everything we thought we knew about joy and happiness upside down. Through updated research and sophisticated brain scans called fMRIs (functional magnetic resonance imaging), we have a much better understanding of this magnificent mass that makes up about three pounds of our total body weight. Interestingly, the twenty principles Paul recommended under the inspiration of the Holy Spirit sync beautifully with that modern understanding of how our brain works. I love it when science authenticates what faith in God's Word has been telling us all along.

There are two ways you can engage with the content of this book. You can read this as you would any other book, taking in what you can when you can. I believe this will be beneficial to you. The alternative is to take this book on as a twenty-five-day challenge.

What might that look like? Over the next twenty-five days, make a commitment to take this journey with me. Let's call it the Joy Challenge. Research shows that engaging in a process like this over just twenty-one days in a row can literally begin to rewire our brains for greater joy and allow our brains to work more optimistically and successfully.[8] That's a pretty good ROI (return on investment). Our challenge spans twenty-five days, to make sure it takes. Here's what the Joy Challenge involves:

- **READ:** There are a total of twenty-five sections, including the four introductory parts that organize the principles, minus this introduction but including the conclusion. When you officially start the challenge, begin by reading the section for that day. The sections are quite short, so it won't take you long. If you are reading one of the four introductory parts, you will be prompted to take some time to journal some personal thoughts in response to the prompt.
- **DO:** You will be given a practical application for each joy principle. Your challenge is to put the principle into practice that day. Then take some time to journal your experience.

- **MEMORIZE:** A key component of this challenge is to "hide" God's Word in your heart (Psalm 119:11). You will be asked to memorize four key passages, one for each of the four chapters of the book of Philippians. You'll find them at the start of each of the introductory parts. Don't worry, they aren't super long, but they are supernaturally powerful to carry around in your mind's pocket.

- **REVIEW:** Before you start the Joy Challenge, go to www.randyfrazee .com/joy-cube to download and print out the Joy Cube, which has all twenty principles on it. Or, you can scan the QR code below. I recommend using cardstock or something with more heft, but you can also use regular paper if that's what you have. The goal here is to keep the Joy Cube with you for all twenty-five days. When you get to your destination, pop it open and make sure you spend time reviewing all twenty principles. It should spark some interesting conversations. Simply tell your inquisitors your story.

- **SHARE:** The final step is to share the Joy Challenge with someone else. Better yet, gift them the experience. Even better yet, agree to do it again with them. You can't have enough joy. Can I get an amen?

When you complete the Joy Challenge, my hope and belief is that you will begin to experience more joy. Real joy that the joy robbers can't steal. And you won't even have to move north where people freeze their tushies off; you won't have to become president of the United States, win a beauty contest, or keep up with the Joneses.

So, are you up for the challenge? If you are, pick your start date (write that date in the space that follows). Count out twenty-five days from your start date—that's your finish date (write this date in the appropriate space that follows). Consider inviting someone to join you in this experience. Doing this with another person or even a small group will greatly increase your probability of success.

Start Date: _____

Finish Date: _____

Let me offer a prayer for you as you embark on this amazing journey:

*Dear God, words do not adequately describe how excited I am for the person holding this book. I don't know them by name, at least not yet, but you do and you long for them to experience joy. Your Son, Jesus, told us that it was his desire for his joy to be complete in us. We know that his joy is real joy, deep and lasting. We can't pray the joy robbers away, but we can overcome them. I pray your vision over this child of yours. I pray courage and discipline over this child of yours. I pray that in the end, your joy is pressed and imprinted on their very souls, and they will tell everyone where this amazing source of joy is found—in you. I pray this with great confidence in the name of Jesus. Amen!*

## THE JOY CHALLENGE SCHEDULE

When you complete a task, check it off the list:

☐ Day 1: Part 1 Joy Despite Your Circumstances
☐ Day 2: Principle #1 Recall Happy Memories

☐ Day 3: Principle #2 Learn How to Love

☐ Day 4: Principle #3 See the Glass as Half-Full

☐ Day 5: Principle #4 Embrace Your No-Lose Situation

☐ Day 6: Principle #5 Take the High Road Without Fear

☐ Day 7: Part 2 Joy Despite People

☐ Day 8: Principle #6 Get on the Same Page with Your Community

☐ Day 9: Principle #7 Elevate Others Above Yourself

☐ Day 10: Principle #8 Stop Being a Grump

☐ Day 11: Principle #9 Celebrate Other People's Success

☐ Day 12: Principle #10 Do Right by Other People

☐ Day 13: Part 3 Joy Despite Your Past

☐ Day 14: Principle #11 Stay Clear of Legalism

☐ Day 15: Principle #12 Recalculate What Really Matters

☐ Day 16: Principle #13 Put the Past Behind You

☐ Day 17: Principle #14 Focus on the Future

☐ Day 18: Principle #15 Surround Yourself with the Right People

☐ Day 19: Part 4 Joy That Defeats Worry

☐ Day 20: Principle #16 Seek Reconciliation in Your Relationships

☐ Day 21: Principle #17 Give What Troubles You to God

☐ Day 22: Principle #18 Rehearse Your Blessings Daily

☐ Day 23: Principle #19 Accept That More Money and Stuff Isn't the Answer

☐ Day 24: Principle #20 Let People Help You

☐ Day 25: Conclusion Wrapping Up the Challenge

# PART 1

# JOY DESPITE YOUR CIRCUMSTANCES

The late Dr. Howard Hendricks, a beloved seminary professor, once shared with his students, of which I was one, that whenever he asked people how they were doing and they responded, "Okay, under the circumstances," he would quip back, "What are you doing under there?"

For most of us, our joy is held hostage by our circumstances. If our circumstances are good, if they meet with our level of expectation and satisfaction, then there is a better chance we will have a positive outlook on life. If we are not happy with the situations happening in our lives, there is a good chance we are anxious and bummed about it all. It's not rocket science.

Here's what makes it tough to navigate our circumstances: there's only so much we can do to change them. There are things we can do to sustain a good set of circumstances—getting a good night's sleep, proper diet and exercise, hanging around good people, making commonsense decisions, showing up for work, keeping our promises, not overcommitting. These are all things within our control. Then there are some things that are outside of our control—the weather, the actions and attitudes of other people, genetics, economic downturns, the death of a loved one, being falsely accused. Solomon made this observation:

> I have seen something else under the sun:
> The race is not to the swift
>     or the battle to the strong,
> nor does food come to the wise
>     or wealth to the brilliant
>     or favor to the learned;
> but time and chance happen to them all.
>                     (Ecclesiastes 9:11)

Earthbound living is a dangerous business; no one can escape this reality no matter who you are. But God set us up for unexpected circumstances. He hardwired us to respond to dangers that threaten us. It is our first response to most all situations we face, designed to keep us safe from harm. Built into our brains is a system governing how we react to fear, driven by an almond-shaped structure in our brain called the *amygdala* that is superfast and doesn't require a ton of rational thought.

Suppose you are walking in the wilderness with friends when a predator—a lion, a grizzly bear, or a tiger—jumps out of nowhere and begins chasing the group. The amygdala kicks into high gear to make an instant choice of fight, flight, or freeze. In this circumstance, you choose flight, and instantly the brain sends a signal to the adrenal gland, located on top of your kidney, to give you an extra boost of energy to run. Adrenaline is released throughout the body. As the old joke goes, the goal is not to be the fastest member of your group but to avoid being the slowest!

Escaping the jaws of a dangerous animal is a good thing, but when we let a fear response dominate our reactions to everyday life circumstances, it can become the greatest enemy of our happiness. Many of us choose to live life from the fear center of our brain all the time, and it robs us of joy. I have been guilty of this in several seasons of my life. But we don't have to live that way. From day one God designed the human brain in such a way that we don't have to live in a state of fear. There is a part of the brain called the *prefrontal cortex*, and it is not only bigger but also way more powerful than the mammalian part of our brain that responds to fear. God has given us the ability to override our fear system and live in a happier place.

This is what the apostle Paul wanted to teach us and even train us to experience—how to rise above our circumstances and live in a continual state of joy. This is God's idea of joy and his desire for our lives. Dr. Larry Richards offered this observation: "Tracing the concept of joy through the Bible helps us realize that our happiness, like our hope, is founded on realities that are unaffected by conditions of this world."[1]

If anyone knew about living in less-than-ideal conditions, the apostle Paul did. Paul's circumstances were up and down (mostly down, by my count). Here is his autobiographical recollection of some of the things he faced in his life:

> I have worked much harder, been in prison more frequently, been
> flogged more severely, and been exposed to death again and again.

Five times I received from the Jews the forty lashes minus one. Three times I was beaten with rods, once I was pelted with stones, three times I was shipwrecked, I spent a night and a day in the open sea, I have been constantly on the move. I have been in danger from rivers, in danger from bandits, in danger from my fellow Jews, in danger from Gentiles; in danger in the city, in danger in the country, in danger at sea; and in danger from false believers. I have labored and toiled and have often gone without sleep; I have known hunger and thirst and have often gone without food; I have been cold and naked. (2 Corinthians 11:23–27)

That's pretty intense, wouldn't you agree? Yet, in his letter to the Philippian believers while under house arrest, he wrote, "I have learned the secret of being content in any and every situation" (Philippians 4:12). And in his letter to the believers in ancient Corinth, he wrote, "In all our troubles my joy knows no bounds" (2 Corinthians 7:4). For Paul, the sky was the limit when it came to joy. In one city, where Paul and his companion Barnabas were ministering, they were persecuted and expelled from the city. Here is what they did in response: "They shook the dust off their feet as a warning to them and went to Iconium. And the disciples were filled with joy and with the Holy Spirit" (Acts 13:51–52). They just shook it off and left filled with joy. That is amazing. This is how I want to respond when people reject or criticize me. Paul's joy quotient was not governed by his circumstances. Joy was a way of life for him.

I want in on this secret.

One scholar wrote this of Paul:

Here one learns that joy is not so much a feeling as it is a settled state of mind characterized by peace, an attitude that views life— including all of its ups and downs—with equanimity. It is a confident way of looking at life that is rooted in faith in the living Lord of the church. For it is possible for one to accept both elation and depression, to accept with creative submission events that bring either delight or dismay, because joy allows one to see beyond any particular event to the sovereign Lord who stands above all events.[2]

Life is 10 percent what happens to you and 90 percent how you react to it.[3] In other words, the driver for our joy is not our external circumstances but how we think about our external circumstances. I don't know about you, but for many years of my life, my joy was attached to my circumstances. When things were good, I was good. But when things changed (as they always do), I was not so good. The shifts were constant—up and down, up and down.

My wife and I had our first child at the start of my graduate studies. I was freaked out about how we were going to make ends meet—joy robber. Our second child was born without a left hand; everything below his left elbow is missing. I had no construct for raising a son with a disability. I struggled to trust in God to give me wisdom for raising him—joy robber. At the age of sixty-two, my mother died of cancer, and I descended into despair—joy robber. Then there were two years of a serious bout with insomnia—joy robber. I was fired twice, leaving me feeling like a failure—definitely a joy robber. I experienced two rounds of betrayal from close friends that threw me into a spiral of clinical depression—yet another joy robber. If you don't mind, I think I'll stop here.

It is likely many of you have had it worse than me. But it is unlikely many of us have had it worse than Paul. He is right up there with Job of the Old Testament on the Richter scale of human earthquakes. The point is not to keep score on who has suffered the most but to focus on who has experienced the most joy despite (or even because of) the suffering.

The kind of joy Paul experienced is not beyond our grasp. The spiritual principles he shared with us, which we'll explore in the following chapters, are attainable—they truly are. Others have learned these principles and have experienced the same brand of resilient joy. Consider these two examples of people who suffered greatly yet found joy beyond their circumstances.

Victor Frankl was a Jewish man who survived the awful concentration camps of Nazi Germany. In his book *Man's Search for Meaning*, Frankl wrote these amazing words:

> We who lived in concentration camps can remember the men who walked through the huts comforting others, giving away their last piece of bread. They may have been few in number, but they offer sufficient proof that everything can be taken from a man but one thing: the last of the human freedoms—to choose one's attitude in any given set of circumstances.[4]

We can also look at Jennifer Rothschild. At the age of fifteen, she was diagnosed with a rare degenerative eye disease that would eventually take her sight. Something she said captured my attention: "It isn't well with my circumstances all the time, but it is forever well with my soul."[5] The external circumstances of her life were dark to say the least. Yet, she found a way to experience peace and contentment on the inside that could weather what life tossed her way on the outside.

This is the pathway Paul wanted to show us in his letter to the church in Philippi. At the end of this, you and I will have a choice to make: to enter onto this path or not. As you might suspect, I said yes and have been applying these concepts for some time. I have not fully arrived, but what I have experienced truly works.

Before you turn the page and start to take in and experience the first of these joy principles, I want to ask you to ponder two things and write your reflections down in a journal:

1. Reflect on the circumstances of your life like Paul did and like I did. Write it out. Then identify where you would place yourself on the Richter scale of human earthquakes: 1.5 is the smallest earthquake; 4.5 is a medium earthquake; 8.5 is a devastating earthquake.
2. Reflect where you would place yourself on a scale of 1 to 10 in terms of your current level of joy: 1–lowest; 10–highest.

What I am really asking is, "How are you doing?" If your response is, "Okay, under the circumstances," I want to ask you, "What are you doing under there?" You don't have to live this way anymore!

> BE SURE TO CARRY YOUR JOY CUBE WITH YOU ALL DAY AND PRACTICE RECITING YOUR FIRST MEMORY VERSE: PHILIPPIANS 1:21.

# RECALL HAPPY MEMORIES

*Paul and Timothy, servants of Christ Jesus,*

*To all God's holy people in Christ Jesus at Philippi, together with the overseers and deacons:*

*Grace and peace to you from God our Father and the Lord Jesus Christ.*

*I thank my God every time I remember you. In all my prayers for all of you, I always pray with joy because of your partnership in the gospel from the first day until now, being confident of this, that he who began a good work in you will carry it on to completion until the day of Christ Jesus.*

*It is right for me to feel this way about all of you, since I have you in my heart and, whether I am in chains or defending and confirming the gospel, all of you share in God's grace with me. God can testify how I long for all of you with the affection of Christ Jesus.*

**–PHILIPPIANS 1:1-8**

In this passage, Paul introduced us to our first principle for increasing our joy despite our circumstances. Notice the word *joy* in verse 4—you could even circle it here or in your Bible. This is the first of sixteen times this word appears in these four short chapters. The lesson here is not explicit but implicit—implied by the attitude and action Paul displayed while chained to a Roman guard, which most would consider to be an awful situation.

Paul was praying "with joy." He was not praying with fear, like most of us would (*Dear God, get me out of this mess*) but with joy because of the good people God put into his life. And by the structure of the grammar, we can see Paul did not wait until his mind happened to remember these people but rather he proactively called them to mind during set prayer times in a day.

Paul was moved by their voluntary partnership with him in his work. The word *partnership* is the Greek word *koinonia* and means "to have something in common." They shared in Paul's burden and his vision given to him by the Lord. It meant the world to Paul.

As far as we know, the church at Philippi was the only church that entered into fellowship with Paul to support his work. Paul didn't like to receive gifts from people he ministered to, for fear someone would accuse him of charging for something that was free. The Philippians knew this and still gave, not once but numerous times over a period of ten years.[1] They convinced him to waive this rule.

Paul used the most intense language he could find to express his deep love and appreciation. In verse 8, he paired his affection with the words "God can testify." In the Revised Standard Version, it translates as, "For God is my witness." Using this phrasing was like taking an oath in a court of law. With your hand on the Bible, you swear to tell the truth, the whole truth, and nothing but the truth, so help you God. Among the Jewish rabbis, swearing such an oath by calling on the name of God was studiously avoided; Paul knew this but did it anyway. He wanted to get his point across, and in his day and in his culture a solemn oath was the end of every dispute.[2]

With God as Paul's witness, he told them he longed for them "with the affection of Christ." The Greek word Paul used for "affection" is the most intense word he could find. It is connected to our English word *visceral*. In New Testament times, this referred to the heart, liver, and lungs, which were regarded as the seat of our deepest-felt emotions. The late British pastor and author F. B. Meyer said, "The Apostle had got so near to the very heart of his Lord that he could hear its throb, detect its beat: nay, it seemed as though the tender mercies of Jesus to these Philippians were throbbing in his own heart."[3] Paul was throwing everything at it he could: "No, I don't think you guys understand how deeply I feel about you and how much joy you bring me."

Paul drove home the point that his joy was not dependent on his circumstances, and yet we find that his joy was affected by his positive relationship with the Philippian believers. It appears they could increase his joy and, at the very least, were capable of not diminishing the amount of joy he possessed. What a gift they were to Paul.

Someone once defined joy as "what I feel when I see the sparkle in someone's eye that conveys 'I'm happy to be with you.'"[4] The Philippians put a sparkle in Paul's eye, and it gave a jolt to his joy. Through his writings, he was now doing the same for them.

## JOY CONDITIONING

When Paul prayed with joy by thanking God for the people in his life, he was recalling happy memories. How exactly does this action increase joy? Dr. Wendy Suzuki, professor of neuroscience and psychology at New York University's Center for Neural Science, offered us some insight through a practice she called *joy conditioning*.[5]

Our brains contain a structure buried deep in our temporal lobe called the *hippocampus*. Its primary job is to file our memories. The more we recall these memories, the stronger they are. Joy conditioning is going back and thinking of a person in your life, recalling the good things they did for you or with you. The more time you spend thinking about it, the stronger this memory gets; and the stronger this memory gets, the more it helps you to overcome the struggles of your current situation and thus increases your joy.

Take a moment now and give it a try. Dr. Suzuki encouraged us to get specific as we revisit the memories, recalling the smells, the sunshine, the fireplace, the words spoken, the music playing. What were the specifics of what the person did for you and how they loved you and believed in you? Maybe take some time to journal about it or put on a song and ruminate on the memory.

Paul chose to engage in joy conditioning during his set prayer times throughout the day. When we pray, particularly when we are feeling anxious, we breathe deeply. When we breathe deeply, the para-sympathetic nervous system in our brains (a network of nerves that relaxes our bodies after periods of stress or danger) decreases our respiration rate and heart rate and shunts blood away from our muscles, which are used for the fear responses of fight or flight, and toward our digestion and reproductive organs. The famous Mayo Clinic tells us that meditation is the most ancient form of medication.[6]

In his prayers perhaps Paul thought of the following:

- the one guy who always had a smile on his face
- the woman who baked him his favorite pie when he came to town
- the teenager who made a courageous decision not to follow the wrong crowd at Philippi High
- the couple who always had something encouraging to say to Paul about his work

- the widow who sacrificed with a heart of joy to contribute to the offering they gave Paul to help him in his work
- the belly laughs shared with a small group of guys sitting around an evening fire

As he relived the experiences in his mind—the sights, the smells, the sounds—he whispered a word of thanks to God for them. When he did this, even though he was chained to a smelly Roman guard, his joy increased, despite his current circumstances.

## THE PHILIPPIANS IN YOUR LIFE

Who are the Philippians in your life? When is the last time you spent time praying with joy by thanking God for them? Scripture and neuroscience tell us that if we make this a habit in our lives, this form of prayer will increase our joy, too, even in the midst of challenging circumstances.

I keep pictures in my office of some of the Philippians in my life. When I look at them, I relive the many encounters we had and, without much effort, I take in a deep breath and exhale a "Thank you, God." I can physically feel my body responding. It is a visceral experience.

One picture I have is of Ray and Mary Graham, who invited me as a fourteen-year-old unchurched boy to their church, which led to my discovery of Jesus. Twenty-seven years later, a member of the church I pastored in Fort Worth, Texas, surprised me by flying them in for the opening of our new building. In the picture I keep in my office, we are wrapping our arms around one another. I consider them my spiritual parents. Even as I write this, tears are streaming down my face. Where would I be today without their invitation? Praying with joy, I thank God for Ray and Mary Graham.

Another picture is of me standing next to a wonderful Christian sociologist by the name of Lyle Schaller. I read all his books while I was in seminary, and they deeply shaped my leadership. Five years into pastoring my first church, I got a chance to meet Lyle personally. For whatever reason, he believed in me and the work I was doing, and it led to my first book contract at the age of thirty-three. A man I looked up to as a giant saw something in me. I recall our lunch meeting repeatedly in my mind. Praying with joy, I thank God for Lyle Schaller.

Then there is the picture of Mike Reilly, who has been in my life for more than thirty years now. The stories are too numerous to share here (he was the one who surprised me with Ray and Mary Graham's visit), but I will reminisce with you about one memory with Mike. About six years ago, I experienced a bout of betrayal that drove me into a state of chronic depression. I called Mike and shared with him that I needed some advice and would like to come visit him over the following weeks. After we hung up, he immediately called me back and said that he'd heard something in my voice that told him I was really struggling. He jumped on a plane at his own expense and was sitting with me in my backyard by noon the next day. By the end of the day, he had not only lifted my spirits but also made a financial contribution to a new adventure for me. I didn't see that coming. Praying with joy, I thank God for Mike Reilly.

Okay, will you indulge me with just one more? I have a picture in my office of a man named Norman Miller. Norman led a company he started from scratch that manages some of the world's greatest Christian recording artists. Back in 2011, he rallied a group of these artists to create a compilation album around a project I architected called The Story (the album is called *The Music Inspired by The Story*). He invited me to tour with these artists at Christmastime. I narrated the story of the Bible in between these artists masterfully singing their songs. It was a "someone pinch me" kind of experience.

One day during the tour, as we were getting on the plane to travel to the next city, Norman looked at me and said, "Randy, I like you." I appropriately said back, "Well, Norm, I like you too." He went on to explain, "Randy, I love a lot of people in my life. I love them unconditionally, because that is what Christ calls me to do. But I don't necessarily like them. I like you. I like being with you." How did that make me feel? Exactly like the definition of joy I presented earlier in this chapter: "What I feel when I see the sparkle in someone's eye that conveys, 'I'm happy to be with you.'"[7] Norman had that sparkle in his eye about me, and it overwhelmed me. Someone was happy with me.

Norman later shared with me that he had a type of blood cancer called multiple myeloma. As we were touring in the middle of our second year, Norman passed away. The very last words he spoke to me from his hospital bed were—you guessed it—"Randy, I like you." Praying with joy, I thank God for Norman Miller.

## THE JOY CHALLENGE

So here is your first Joy Challenge. Let's call it the Gratitude Visit.[8] Follow these steps:

1. Identify the Philippians in your life. I encourage you to write their names down. If you have time, you might want to display a picture of them like I do.
2. Identify one person on your list who is still alive who you never properly thanked. Pick someone you can meet with today, either in person or over a video call (preferably in person).
3. Write a letter of gratitude. It should be about three hundred words in length and should be very specific about how they

positively affected your life. Like Paul, don't be afraid to use extreme language to get your point across.

4. Reach out to the person and let them know you want to meet up with them sometime today, no later than tomorrow. Be vague about the purpose of the meeting.

5. Before you meet, get in a quiet place to pray. If a song of nostalgia comes to mind, play it. Close your eyes and breathe deeply in and out several times as you relive the memory of how they impacted your life. At the end of your prayer, whisper to God how thankful you are for the person and pray for any needs they may have.

6. Meet with the person and simply read your letter, word for word. Let them see that sparkle in your eye that tells them how happy you are with them.

7. Before the day closes, journal about your experience.

BE SURE TO CARRY YOUR JOY CUBE WITH YOU ALL DAY AND PRACTICE RECITING YOUR FIRST MEMORY VERSE: PHILIPPIANS 1:21.

# PRINCIPLE #2

# LEARN HOW TO LOVE

*And this is my prayer: that your love may abound more and more in knowledge and depth of insight, so that you may be able to discern what is best and may be pure and blameless for the day of Christ, filled with the fruit of righteousness that comes through Jesus Christ—to the glory and praise of God.*

–PHILIPPIANS 1:9-11

Paul opened his wonderful letter to the Philippian believers by telling them he was praying for them and reminiscing about the wonderful memories he had with them, which was helping him rise above the challenges of his current circumstances. Then Paul told them specifically how he was praying for them. It is in the content of his prayer that we are introduced to our second joy principle. The singular focus of his prayer was that they would learn how to love.

What we are going to see from Paul's instruction is that when we learn how to love people better, not only does other people's joy increase, but so does ours.

In the Old Testament, the high priest wore a special garment called the *ephod*. It was a beautiful breastplate made of "gold, and of blue, purple and scarlet yarn, and of finely twisted linen" (Exodus 28:6). Mounted into the breastplate were twelve precious stones, one for each of the twelve tribes of Israel. The name of the family was engraved in each stone. Why? In Exodus 28:29, God gives this instruction: "Whenever Aaron [the high priest] enters the Holy Place, he will bear the names of the sons of Israel over his heart." I love that. And Paul did the same thing. As he entered the "holy place" for his daily prayers, he carried the names of the Philippian believers over his heart as he remembered them and asked for the blessing of growth on their behalf.

He prayed that their "love would abound more and more" (Philippians 1:9). The word *abound* in the Greek language means "more than enough." He wanted them to have so much love inside them that they would have no place to store it.[1] They would have no choice but to let it spill out of them to others.

He wanted their love to grow in "knowledge and depth of insight" (v. 9). The word *knowledge* deals with the general principles of love, while "depth of insight" deals with its application.[2] Love is not lackadaisical or unsophisticated. There are principles that drive the art of love, and believers need to be fluent in them. Learning how to love takes a great deal of focus and training.

For example, one general principle of love is the necessity of simply acknowledging another person's existence. This can be done by choosing to look another person in the eyes when you encounter them. Neuroscience tells us that when we engage in this simple act it triggers a feeling of affinity and togetherness. We should do this for everyone. Why not? Such a simple act, but what a powerful result.

What about the "depth of insight" Paul prayed for? I believe this refers to our knowledge about how to transfer the general principles of love best to the specific people God has placed in our lives. With the encouraging words we speak, for example, we can avoid being generic and demonstrate that we have history with that person, like applying healing ointment on a wound because we know their story and where it hurts. Likewise, the gifts we give can be more than standard, revealing that we truly have insight into the nuances of what brings a smile to that person's face.

What is the reason for this customized kind of love? "So that you may be able to discern what is best and may be pure and blameless for the day of Christ" (Philippians 1:10).

Our love needs to be pure. The word *pure* also translates as "sincere." It is a compound word in the Greek, meaning both "sunlight" and "judgment." In those days, many artisans would use colored wax to hide cracks and chips in their pottery and sculptures. You could tell if wax was used by holding the piece up to the sunlight. Artisans who refrained from the practice allegedly marked their pieces with a stamp that read "*sine cera*," which means "without wax."[3] Mature love comes without adding wax. It has no need to use manipulating flattery or backhanded compliments, for example, to cover up the cracks of ulterior motives. Rather, we are called to a love that is pure.

Our love needs to be "blameless." This means our love must not be offensive. Our love should not cause people to stumble. Immature love often rides another person so hard it crushes their spirit. We might want the best for them, but our approach is harmful in the end. This reminds me of the phenomenon of *helicopter parents*, a term that has been used since the late 1980s to describe parents who hover over their children in a destructively intrusive manner. The care and attention of a helicopter parent ends up being counterproductive, often causing difficulties for the child in the long term. It turns out the primary driver of helicopter parenting is a desire to build up the parents' identity and mask their fears, rather than genuine love for the child.

On the other hand, sometimes our immature love lets too many things slide—we turn a blind eye to destructive behavior. Proverbs 27:6 offers this instruction: "Faithful are the wounds of a friend" (NKJV). Sometimes, not often, God calls us, based on the trust we have earned over time, to confront our friends, "speaking the truth in love" (Ephesians 4:15). In Paul's letter to the Galatian believers, he wrote, "If someone is caught in a sin, you who live by the Spirit should restore that person gently" (6:1). So, for our love to be blameless, to be a mature kind of love, it needs to be one that lifts people up and helps them find firm footing, even and perhaps especially when they are caught up in potentially harmful choices.

Paul then continued the passage in Philippians by throwing in this line: "for the day of Christ" (v. 10). What does this mean? It refers to the day when Jesus returns to the earth to establish his eternal kingdom. When Jesus returns, we want him to catch us in the act of loving people sincerely. Since the "day of Christ" might be today, we want to stay in a perpetual state of Spirit-led love. This expression of love is a tricky business.

Paul wrapped up this passage by identifying the source of this healthy brand of love. We are to be "filled with the fruit of righteousness that comes through Jesus Christ" (v. 11). We are not offering love that comes from us. Our human-produced love is tainted by our past and filled with mixed motives, codependency, competition, jealousy, and a lack of knowledge. Rather, we are to allow the pure nutrients of *agape*[4] love to flow from Christ into our branches so that the fruit on the tree of our life that others taste is the sweet and refreshing flavor of unconditional and sacrificial love.

Think of our lives like a glass of wine made from the fruit of the vine. The varietal is not Cabernet Sauvignon or Pinot Grigio but love.

This is what Paul tells us in Galatians 5:22: "The fruit of the Spirit is love." When people taste a glass of Cabernet, they often pick up the flavors that define that wine. They may taste hints of cinnamon, blackberry, or even pencil lead. When people take a drink of genuine agape love, the first hint they will pick up on is joy. When our lives are filled with joy, others can enjoy the time they spend with us. When we proactively love them, we transfer our joy to them.

Paul finished this passage by giving us our ultimate motive. We daily stay connected to the vine of Christ, not for our own sake but for the sake of others and "to the glory and praise of God" (Philippians 1:11).

## HOW LOVE INCREASES JOY

How does learning to love others work to increase our joy? Let's go back to the teaching of Jesus in John 15. Jesus informed us that the love the Father has for him he passed on to us. He then offered us a command: "Love one another as I have loved you" (v. 12 NKJV). When we take in more and more of God's love for us, it spills out of us to others. It is God's love we offer to those around us versus the sometimes toxic love that comes from humans alone.

Just before this Jesus said, "I have told you this so that *my joy* may be in you and that *your joy* may be complete" (v. 11, emphasis added). When we complete this chain reaction of godly love passed from the Father to the Son to and through us, our joy increases. Why? When we taste God's brand of love, we pick up strong hints of his joy. One scholar on the life of Paul wrote, "People who know how to love are filled with joy."[5] Eureka!

Once again, research agrees with Jesus. Harvard University has done what they dubbed "The World's Longest Scientific Study of Happiness."[6] This eighty-five-year study began in 1938 with 268 sophomore boys from Harvard. They also added to the study a group of 456 fourteen-year-old boys from troubled families and disadvantaged neighborhoods in Boston. Researchers followed these 724 boys from adolescence and young adulthood into their eighties, seeking to discover one thing: the secret to joy and happiness. The assumption, of course, was that the Harvard boys were set up way better for a happier life than the boys who came from a difficult or less privileged upbringing.

So, what did they discover was the secret to happiness? Money or fame or pleasure or power? Not even close. Are you ready? Wait for it. The key to happiness and joy is love. Despite the boys' external circumstances, the number-one predictor of whether they were among the healthiest and happiest people in their eighties was the presence of loving relationships.

The authors of the study concluded, "If we had to take all eighty-five years of the Harvard study and boil it down to a single principle for living, one life investment that is supported by similar findings across a variety of other studies, it would be this: Good relationships keep us healthier and happier. Period."[7]

When they interviewed the test subjects, they discovered that loving relationships buffered the ups and downs of the pain experienced in the later years of life. In other words, the experience of healthy love enabled people to enjoy happiness despite their circumstances. Love, as it turns out, is the most powerful medicine available to us.

As we might suspect, the research shows a lack of joy for people who are starved of the wonderful dance of giving and receiving love. Isolation and loneliness are associated with greater sensitivity to pain, suppression of the immune system, diminished brain function, and less effective sleep. In fact, loneliness in older people is twice as unhealthy as obesity and increases the odds of death in any given year by 26 percent.[8]

Here's the deal: When we are alone, our brains know that we are more vulnerable, and it puts our bodies into survival mode. Stress hormones are released—not good. If we stay in this state of being for an extended period, it takes its toll on our minds, our bodies, and our souls. We become stressed out—not a good recipe for joy.

# LOVE LETTERS

When our four children were young, they used to buy me presents on Father's Day. I would get the standard tie or even the dreaded "soap on a rope" (which I'm not sure they make anymore, so younger people may have to Google it). To add insult to injury, to purchase a gift they used my money—joy robber.

So, when my children were still quite young, I went to them and said, "What I really, really would like more than anything is a hand-written note from you on how you are doing and how you feel about our relationship." This year, my oldest child, our daughter, turns forty years old, and I still receive notes from all my children. Now I also receive them from my grandchildren.

Today, I don't have any of the ties they gave me, and I never used the soap on a rope (I think I regifted them), but I have every single letter they have given me. Let me share just one I received recently from one of our four adult children:

> You were and are an amazing father. Every time you hear a reference to something you taught and showed us growing up, know there are thousands beyond that one that you don't see or hear that is impacting our lives and others in our lives. Thanks for being intentional and personal about your involvement in our lives. We all received the same lessons, but you tailored that teaching and lesson to each

of us, so we heard it and grew from it (even if it didn't seem like we heard it at the time).

My children have learned how to love their dad well. These letters bring me pure joy. But if Paul and modern science got it right, it also brings my children joy. To know that they are in a unique position of intimacy with me and that, through their depth of insight about me, they can craft a few words that send my joy meter through the roof, well, that is a source of joy for them, for sure.

## THE JOY CHALLENGE

Your Joy Challenge today is to learn to love better. Love is something we long for, but loving others does not come naturally to us. One of the many aspects of learning how to love better is pinpointing the love language of the people God has placed in our lives. We all receive love differently. The key is discovering how the people around us best receive love. Author Gary Chapman gives us the best list of love languages I have seen:[9]

- **GIFTS:** the giving of a thoughtful or nice gift.
- **SERVICE:** doing something for the other person; taking something off their to-do list.
- **WORDS:** offering thoughtful words that tell the person how you feel about them and how you appreciate them.
- **TOUCH:** giving physical affection, such as a big bear hug or letting the person rest his or her head in the crevice of your shoulder or holding their hand or giving them a back rub.
- **QUALITY TIME:** choosing to spend time with the person over something else you like to do.

Let's take some time to exercise what we've learned about employing love languages. Here are the steps to your next challenge:

1. Identify your love language. How do you like to receive love? My top love language is "Words," for example.
2. Identify one person God has placed in your life to love. You might write their name down in your journal.
3. Identify their love language. You can guess, ask some others who know them well, or simply ask them yourself. Most of us love according to what works for us. A learned lover knows what your love language is and loves you accordingly. They become fluent in your love language.
4. Ask God to give you a simple way to show this person love according to their love language by the end of the day. It's okay to get some help from others if they can keep it a secret. Write your idea down in your journal.
5. Love them.
6. Before the day closes, write about your experience. Did this act bring joy to the person? Did it bring joy to you? Be specific.

BE SURE TO CARRY YOUR JOY CUBE WITH YOU ALL DAY AND PRACTICE RECITING YOUR FIRST MEMORY VERSE: PHILIPPIANS 1:21.

# PRINCIPLE #3

# SEE THE GLASS
# AS HALF-FULL

*Now I want you to know, brothers and sisters, that what has happened to me has actually served to advance the gospel. As a result, it has become clear throughout the whole palace guard and to everyone else that I am in chains for Christ. And because of my chains, most of the brothers and sisters have become confident in the Lord and dare all the more to proclaim the gospel without fear.*

*It is true that some preach Christ out of envy and rivalry, but others out of goodwill. The latter do so out of love, knowing that I am put here for the defense of the gospel. The former preach Christ out of selfish ambition, not sincerely, supposing that they can stir up trouble for me while I am in chains. But what does it matter? The important thing is that in every way, whether from false motives or true, Christ is preached. And because of this I rejoice.*

–PHILIPPIANS 1:12-18

Circle the word *rejoice* at the end of verse 18. Paul shared with us from verses 12 through 18 something that caused him to rejoice: the opportunities afforded to him and the gospel because he was imprisoned. This is absolutely nuts. There are a lot of things that evoke a joyful response in me, but what Paul was experiencing wouldn't be one of them. Wouldn't you agree? Let's probe a little deeper to discover the third secret to increasing our joy despite our circumstances.

Paul began by sharing with the Philippian believers this assurance: "Now I want you to know, brothers and sisters, that what has happened to me has actually served to advance the gospel" (v. 12). He just glossed over "what has happened to him," but he had been through the wringer and back. If it were me, I would have spent several pages spewing out all the wrongs I had suffered. Perhaps that's why I wasn't selected to write the treatise on joy.

But this is why Paul experienced more joy than the rest of us do. As the adage goes, we see the glass as half-empty, whereas Paul saw the glass as half-full. This is the heart and soul of the next principle for increasing our joy despite our circumstances. It wasn't that Paul looked at the world through rose-colored glasses. His gaze was focused on something different. We are naturally focused on ourselves; Paul was focused on the mission. He did not find his joy in ideal circumstances but in seeing people find hope in Jesus.

The word *advance* in verse 12 means "pioneer advance." It is a Greek military term referring to the army of engineers who go before the troops to open the way into new territory.[1] Paul discovered his circumstances opened the way for the message of Christ to go to the world through the mighty influence of Rome. Paul's imprisonment gave him an audience he would not otherwise have had. As a Roman citizen, because he made his appeal to the emperor, Paul was the emperor's prisoner (although Paul preferred to think of himself as "the prisoner of Jesus").[2] As a consequence, Paul was guarded twenty-four hours a day, seven days a week by a member of the palace guard. Some suggest that Paul was chained to the soldiers. Who were these guys? They were the emperor's bodyguards. They would change shifts every four hours. That means that Paul would have had a captive audience for four hours at a time with six different guards every day.

As a pastor, if I am lucky, I get thirty minutes a week with my audience, and they are certainly not chained to me. They can—and do—walk out on me sometimes. But Paul's guards couldn't do that. No doubt, once their shifts ended, these influential guards were talking with others and sharing in the praetorian barracks about their experiences with this extraordinary prisoner and his teachings. The gospel was spreading, and that brought Paul joy.

But it didn't end here. On his long journey to Rome, Paul had the opportunity to speak in the presence of two Roman governors (Felix and Festus), King Herod Agrippa,[3] and these rulers' wives. Over a span of two years, Governor Felix regularly sent for Paul from his prison cell to converse with him. Each time Paul presented his case, it forced the court officials to study the doctrines and claims of the Christian faith. And now he was awaiting his opportunity to share his message in front of Nero, the mighty emperor of Rome.

When Paul first became a follower of Jesus on the road to Damascus, he was told by the Lord through a man named Ananias that he would suffer and speak in front of kings (Acts 9:15–16). That day had come, and Paul was rejoicing.

You would think Paul's circumstances would cause other believers to back down from their witness. After all, they could have been next to be thrown in prison. But that was not the case. Rather, Paul's response to his circumstances inspired them. Little did the Romans realize that the chains they affixed to Paul's wrists would release him to accomplish his mission instead of binding him.[4]

Give me the same set of circumstances Paul had, and I'd be

thinking about how awful prison food was. But Paul was thinking of the opportunity to dish out the eternally nourishing food of the gospel. I'd be thinking of how wrong this whole affair was; Paul was thinking about how right this opportunity was to share his message of life. I'd be thinking about how discouraged I was; Paul was thinking about how this had encouraged followers everywhere to share their faith. Paul thought differently than we do. And Paul likely experienced more joy than we do.

Paul wrote that he was experiencing joy in spite of his critics (Philippians 1:17–18).[5] Paul's chains not only inspired his base, but they also motivated some bandits. He was super popular, even though that was not what he was striving for. In today's world of social media influencers, Paul would definitely have the blue check mark next to his Instagram and X (formerly Twitter) accounts. Paul was crazy successful. By the end of his life, he had planted ten churches, encouraged hundreds of other churches, and penned thirteen of the twenty-seven books of the New Testament. This is a recipe for jealousy.

There were other Christian leaders who saw Paul's imprisonment as a chance to make their mark. They were making their move to become the next celebrity evangelist. Some things never change. Malevolency has always been a thing. So, what was Paul's response to these goons moving in on his territory? He wrote, "But what does it matter? The important thing is that in every way, whether from false motives or true, Christ is preached" (v. 18).

Paul's joy wasn't wrapped up in his popularity. Seeing the mission advance is what fueled his joy. While these knuckleheads' motives were way out of line, they were apparently teaching the true gospel—they were getting it right. This meant the mission was being accomplished. Paul saw his imprisonment as a multiplier. As an individual, he could get only so much done. His circumstances motivated others to step it up, which exponentially expanded the work. To Paul, this was a good thing.

New Testament scholar F. F. Bruce wrote,

There is a striking similarity between Paul's attitude here and Luther's often-quoted words from the preface to the Letter of James in his German New Testament of 1522: "That which does not teach Christ is not apostolic, even if Peter or Paul taught it. Again, that which does preach Christ is apostolic, even if Judas, Annas, Pilate or Herod did it." What matters is the content of the preaching, not the identity of the preacher.[6]

My church history professor from seminary once told the class, after surveying the motives of Christian leaders throughout the centuries, "If on any given day your motives are 60 percent pure, it's a good day." Paul knew this about humanity. He likely spotted imperfections in his own life. He factored this into his overall assessment of the situation. When Paul looked at his circumstances, he saw the glass as half-full. And when he did this, it caused him to rejoice.

## YOUR BRAIN AND POSITIVITY

Modern discoveries in neuroscience know why Paul's attitude increased his joy. Shawn Achor, author of *The Happiness Advantage*, informed us that when our brain is positive it is 31 percent more productive than when our brain is focused on the negative. When we have "the glass is half-full" mentality about our life circumstances, our brain releases a shot of dopamine.

Dopamine acts as a chemical messenger, communicating between nerve cells in our brain and the rest of our body. This transaction serves two positive functions: it not only makes us happier; it also turns on the learning centers in our brain, allowing us to adapt to the world in a different way—including when we're experiencing negative circumstances, such as being in prison or having other people take advantage of you.[7]

But that is not all. Brain expert Dr. Daniel Amen wrote, "People who say they have few positive experiences on a daily basis have higher levels of inflammation. Being able to point to frequent moments of positivity throughout the day is associated with lower levels of inflammation."[8] When our negative thoughts about our circumstances get out of control, we send our body into stress. To combat this stress, our immune system proteins create inflammation to surround and protect the body and brain. If this stress is not controlled over time, the inflammation can lead to the hardening of the arteries and cardiovascular disease.[9] When inflammation is high, it "ignites a long list of other disorders: arthritis, asthma, atherosclerosis, blindness, cancer, diabetes, and, quite possibly, autism and mental illness."[10] None of that sounds good to me.

Bottom line: toxic thinking wears down the brain; optimism fires up the brain to maximum joy. Paul experienced this when he wrote his letter around AD 62. Modern neuroscience now confirms it to be true 1,960 years later. As the old adage goes, "Better late than never."

## BEING A POLLYANNA

For years I've heard people say, "Oh, that's Pollyanna" in response to people looking on the bright side of things. By this they mean the comment made was naïve, out of touch with the harsh realities of life. As it turns out, this is not what it means at all. *Pollyanna* is a classic Disney film released in May 1960 (eight months before my arrival to this world). The film was adapted from a 1920 novel about an orphan daughter of missionaries who was sent to live with her wealthy, stern aunt.

When Pollyanna was younger, her dad created the Glad Game after she received a pair of crutches in the mail for Christmas instead of the doll she wanted. Given this negative circumstance, the game invited her to identify something positive from it. So instead of being sullen or disappointed that she hadn't received her desired doll, Pollyanna decided she was grateful she didn't need the crutches.

As the movie unfolds, she has numerous opportunities to play the Glad Game, given her circumstances. When her mean aunt punished her for being late for dinner by downgrading her dinner each night to bread and water, Pollyanna decided that bread and water were her favorite meal. When her aunt banished her to a room in the attic with no pictures, rugs, or mirror, Pollyanna decided she would look out the window at the beautiful trees instead, which she deemed much better than pictures on a wall.

One Sunday afternoon, Pollyanna was in the backyard while her aunt, the cook, and a pair of maids griped and complained about the pastor's hellfire-and-brimstone sermon from that morning. Pollyanna tried her best to brighten the mood with her alternative attitude, but on that day, she got pushback. One of the maids challenged her: "Alright, Miss Smarty-Pants, what's so good about Sunday?" Pollyanna thought for a moment, and then she replied, "You can be glad because . . . because it will be six whole days before Sunday comes around again." That one hits close to home for me as a pastor! But I love her positive spin on such a dismal experience.

Allow me to throw in another story to drive the point home. A father was surprised at the difference in the dispositions of his two sons. One was a confirmed optimist and the other a pessimist. He decided to test and see how far they would carry these traits. On Christmas morning, the two boys came downstairs to see what Santa had brought them. The father hid behind the door and watched them. In one boy's stocking was only a piece of leather halter and a small horsewhip. The other boy's stocking was overflowing with gifts. This latter boy, who was the pessimist, looked over his array of presents with a bit of sadness. "What did you get?" asked his cheerful brother. "Not much, just the usual—games and things—nothing I really care about. How about you?" The optimist replied, "I got a pony, but it ran away."

Paul, Pollyanna, and this little boy simply looked for the good around them, rather than looking for what was wrong. If we want joy despite our circumstances, we would do well to do the same.

## THE JOY CHALLENGE

Consciously directing your thoughts is a stiff challenge, but I think it is a worthy one. So here is your Joy Challenge for practicing this joy principle of seeing the glass as half-full. As you go through the day, find situations where you can apply Paul's famous question: "But what does it matter?" The opportunities abound. Let me give you one common example. Let's say you are driving down the freeway and somebody cuts you off at an exit. Normally, you might say . . . well, I better not write down what you or I might normally say. This time I want you to shake it off and say (go ahead and say it out loud), "But what does it matter?"

Don't stop there. Look for the angle. Instead of assuming the guy (or gal) is a jerk, ponder a different scenario. Maybe they are new to your city and are lost—they didn't mean to cut you off; they likely didn't even see you. It happens to the best of us. You don't want their first couple of days in your city to make them think it is filled with impatient jerks. Then maybe whisper this prayer, "Thank you, God, that no one got hurt." And if your children are in the back seat, you will be modeling for them this valuable principle on increasing your joy despite your circumstances.

## SEE THE GLASS AS HALF-FULL

Look for three opportunities today to practice this principle. Then, at the end of the day, take some time to journal your thoughts.

BE SURE TO CARRY YOUR JOY CUBE WITH YOU ALL DAY AND PRACTICE RECITING YOUR FIRST MEMORY VERSE: PHILIPPIANS 1:21.

# EMBRACE YOUR NO-LOSE SITUATION

*Yes, and I will continue to rejoice, for I know that through your prayers and God's provision of the Spirit of Jesus Christ what has happened to me will turn out for my deliverance. I eagerly expect and hope that I will in no way be ashamed, but will have sufficient courage so that now as always Christ will be exalted in my body, whether by life or by death. For to me, to live is Christ and to die is gain. If I am to go on living in the body, this will mean fruitful labor for me. Yet what shall I choose? I do not know! I am torn between the two: I desire to depart and be with Christ, which is better by far; but it is more necessary for you that I remain in the body. Convinced of this, I know that I will remain, and I will continue with all of you for your progress and joy in the faith, so that through my being with you again your boasting in Christ Jesus will abound on account of me.*

**–PHILIPPIANS 1:18–26**

Paul opened our fourth joy principle by writing, "Yes, and I will continue to rejoice." In our last chapter Paul was choosing to rejoice in the midst of a very difficult situation. Here we find him at it again, continuing to say yes to the opportunity to rejoice despite his circumstances. By now we expect Paul to say this. But what we wouldn't anticipate is the content that follows. This is the grand-daddy of joy principles and even contains our recommended Scripture memory verse for the week, verse 21. If we can grab hold of this principle and truly incorporate it into our lives, our joy will go to another stratosphere. What is it? Paul was embracing his no-lose situation. Allow me to explain.

He began by giving the reason for his uninterrupted joy: "For I know that through your prayers and God's provision of the Spirit of Jesus Christ what has happened to me will turn out for my deliverance" (v. 19). Paul was quoting verbatim the words of Job of the Old Testament, the guy who lost everything he had in a day (Job 13:16). Paul understood and interpreted his situation like Job did. As Job was ultimately saved from his plight and vindicated, so Paul ultimately experienced the same. Thus, he was able to say "I know" with a conviction originating in sacred scripture.[1]

Paul based his confidence in his deliverance on two things. First, the Philippian believers prayed for him. Paul believed in the effectiveness of prayer because he had witnessed its power many times. Paul prayed daily for them (1:4), and it turns out they were praying daily for Paul. The word used here and in verse 4 is not the normal word for prayer. In its original meaning, the word connotes "lack" or "need." It is a kind of prayer where the intercessor is very specific in their request for another person. What a blessing to be the recipient of this kind of prayer, tailor-made to his unique circumstances.

The second reason for his confidence comes from the assurance he felt from the Holy Spirit within him. In verse 20, he told them, "I eagerly expect and hope that I will in no way be ashamed, but will have sufficient courage." The words *eagerly expect* carry the idea of an Olympic runner whose head is outstretched, straining forward, and ignoring everyone else on the track. Paul was pumped with purpose. He saw the finish line and intended to break through it as the victor.

What was Paul's desired outcome after this whole thing was over? First, that he would in no way be ashamed. He was no doubt thinking of delivering his message to Nero. He knew Jesus would be watching, and it was Jesus—and Jesus alone—whom he wanted to please. He had come too far to back down when it was go time.

But then Paul expressed his ultimate purpose: in the end, he wanted to make sure Jesus was exalted in and through his body, whether dead or alive. The word *exalted* translates as "magnified" in other translations. It means "to make something large." The late Bible teacher Warren Wiersbe put it this way:

> The telescope brings distant things closer, and the microscope makes tiny things look big. To the unbeliever, Jesus is not very big. Other people and other things are far more important. But as the unbeliever watches Christians go through a crisis experience, he ought to be able to see how big Jesus really is. The believer's body is a lens that makes a "little Christ" look very big, and a "distant Christ" come very close.[2]

This is what Paul had in mind. Whether this experience left him dead or alive, it made no difference to Paul, as long as his mission to exalt Christ was accomplished. And here was the secret sauce of Paul's joy in this terrible, life-threatening scenario. He saw that he was in a no-lose situation. If Nero cut off his head or if he lived and got to return to Philippi and give those wonderful people a big bear hug, it didn't matter. Either way, Paul won.

"For to me, to live is Christ," Paul wrote (v. 21). What does that mean? It means Paul saw the purpose of his life and his mission completely wrapped up in the person of Christ. That was what the breaths divinely afforded him were for. If Paul made it out of this one alive, he would continue to serve the purposes Jesus had given him to fulfill. In verse 25, he stated the purpose specifically: "I will continue with all of you for your progress and joy in the faith." Here we find the word *progress* again that we saw in verse 12, which means "pioneer advance." With more time, Paul opened fresh new paths to the Philippian believers to increase their joy through their faith. How would you like to have the apostle Paul as your personal joy trainer?

However, if it was God's will for Paul to lose his life for this cause, then Paul saw this as a great gain for him. Why? Death would be a relief from all his hardships—imprisonment, afflictions, beatings, stoning, weariness, pain, privation, and dangers of every sort.[3] Paul found his life a heavy load to carry. Theologian Gerald Hawthorne suggested these "are the words of the very human Paul giving vent to a very human and universal sentiment: death is a gain to those whose life has become weighed down with well-nigh unbearable burdens."[4] Yet, for Paul it was much more than a release from his earthly troubles. He was going to be with Jesus. Paul sensed Christ's real presence in his life on earth, but death would take this sense and move it into reality—he would be with Christ. He was in a no-lose situation, and this was cause for joy, not fear. Paul was not falling down but falling up—a big difference!

## COPING WITH HOPE

Why does embracing our no-lose situation as Christians work to produce greater joy in us? Bottom line, because we can cope with hope. We can cope with the hardships of life and the fear of death when we have the confidence of a better life forever in eternity. One scholar on the life of Paul wrote,

> Over and over again, Paul links joy with the Christian hope . . . such hope can keep a believer joyful, for it includes not only the expectation of the coming of the deliverer, the Lord Jesus Christ, to transfigure our physical bodies, but also assures us joy in the world to come.[5]

If I am going into a situation where I know I cannot lose, I don't lose any sleep over it. Every believer in Jesus has this in their toolbox of faith. The key is to keep this truth ever present in your mind. If you do, your joy will increase.

Throughout his letter, Paul also invited the reader to have a deeper definition of true joy. I love the way Dr. Hawthorne put it:

> For Paul joy is more than a mood or an emotion. Joy is an understanding of existence that encompasses both elation and depression, that can accept with creative submission events which bring delight or dismay because joy allows one to see beyond any particular event to the sovereign Lord who stands above all events and ultimately has control over them. Joy, to be sure, "includes within itself readiness for martyrdom" but equally, the opportunity to go on living and serving.[6]

Our joy rests in the confidence that God will keep his promise to us through our faith in Jesus, no matter the earthly outcome. It's not dependent on the exhausting lifestyle of attempting to manipulate our circumstances so we never experience a trial that might bring us down. It's wholly based on our faith in the one who is trustworthy above all. This is what Paul was getting at, and he really wanted us to grab hold of it.

# RESPONDING TO THE WORST
# THAT COULD HAPPEN

What did focusing on our ultimate purpose and embracing our no-lose situation look like in the early church? Renowned sociologist Dr. Rodney Stark, in his research on how Christianity grew from the one person (Jesus) to more than 33 million people (or 56.5 percent of the entire Western world) in just three short centuries, noted that one of the drivers for the explosive growth of the Jesus movement was how the believers responded during two epidemics that broke out during this period. The first epidemic was in AD 165 and is believed to have been an outbreak of smallpox. The second was in AD 250 and was likely measles. In both cases, one-quarter to one-third of the population of the Western world died. When you compare that to the .0004 percent of people who have died from COVID, the numbers are staggering and socially catastrophic.[7]

Reading historical accounts, Stark discovered that Christians responded very differently from their pagan counterparts. At the first sign of the disease, the pagans threw their family members out in the street to avoid getting infected. Take a look at what Dionysius, a convert of Paul and the first bishop of Athens,[8] wrote in AD 250 as he watched this unfold:

> At the first onset of the disease, they pushed the sufferers away and fled from their dearest, throwing them into the roads before they were dead and treated unburied corpses as dirt, hoping thereby to avert the spread and contagion of the fatal disease; but do what they might, they found it difficult to escape.[9]

The Christians, on the other hand, decided to love and nurse the members of their families back to health, even in the absence of any medicine or a vaccine. But they didn't stop there, Stark reported. They went out into the streets and brought the sick pagans into their homes to love on them in the same manner, even though these people despised Christians. Dionysius shared what he observed among the Christians:

> Most of our brother Christians showed unbounded love and loyalty, never sparing themselves and thinking only of one another. Heedless of danger, they took charge of the sick, attending to their every need and ministering to them in Christ, and with them departed this life serenely happy; for they were infected by others with the disease, drawing on themselves the sickness of their neighbors and cheerfully accepting their pains. Many, in nursing and curing others, transferred their death to themselves and died in their stead.[10]

I don't know about you, but this depth of unconditional love overwhelms me, particularly in light of how intensely we quarantined during our recent pandemic to keep ourselves from one another. I'm not sure I possess this depth of faith and devotion, particularly to people who don't like me.

How did Christianity grow as a result of these believers' courageous response? Stark cited two prominent reasons. First, pagans flocked to the church. Why, of course. What kind of family do you want to be part of, the kind that throws you into the streets at the first sniffle or the family that won't ever abandon you?

There was a second reason we know now that the people back then did not know. Stark wrote, "Modern medical experts believe that conscientious nursing without any medications could cut the mortality rate by two-thirds or even more."[11] When a sick person knows that someone loves them and is willing to risk their life for them, it does something to create healing in the body. When a sick person is looked in the eyes as a being worth saving and is given a blanket, offered a kind word, and caressed with gentle love, it releases a healing agent in their body that goes to work to fight the disease. Love, as it turns out, can be more powerful than a virus. Jesus knew this would happen, because he made us that way. In the end, more Christians survived the viruses than those who did not, and the church grew!

The question many of us might ask in response to this story is, How did the early Christians find the courage to do this? Stark declared that they believed the teachings of Jesus, even though they didn't have a full copy of the Bible in their hands to personally study in those days. When Jesus said that God loved them, they believed it and embraced it. When Jesus told them to not only love their neighbor but to love their enemy, they believed it and lived it out. When Jesus told them that, if they would believe in him, they would inherit eternal life, they believed it with all their heart.

So, when they took in the pagans and nursed them as their own family, they thought, *What's the worst thing that could happen to me? I could die and go be with Jesus.* "To live is Christ . . . to die is gain."

You see what they did? They embraced their no-lose situation. What a way to live.

## THE JOY CHALLENGE

Being the granddaddy of all the joy principles, this one might take a while to grab hold of. That's okay. Let's commit to moving in that direction one day at a time. As we do, we will see our joy increase despite our circumstances.

Here is our Joy Challenge to move us a little closer. Positive psychology has a useful exercise called *decatastrophizing*. It is "a form of cognitive reappraisal" that can help us think differently about what appears at first glance to be catastrophic, a shifting of our mindset that can reduce our stress and thus increase our joy.[12] Get some time alone to ponder the questions below. Write your answers in a journal or in a notes app in your phone. Here's the good news: our no-lose situation Christ has placed us in through our faith applies to any area where we could be riddled with fear.

1. What creates the most fear in you today? (It could be death but also a host of other things, such as financial insecurity, being alone, being in crowds, performing, and illness.) On a scale of 1 to 10, how fearful are you today? (1–not much, 10–extremely). Explain your answer.

2. How likely is what you fear going to happen today or in the near future?

3. What if it were going to happen sooner than later? What is the worst that would happen? (Write this as though a friend is saying this to you.)

4. On a scale of 1 to 10, how firmly do you embrace Paul's attitude, "for to me, to live is Christ and to die is gain" (1–not at all; 10–all in)? What would it take for you to move closer to "all in" on that scale?

5. Share your answers today with at least one other person.

The act of dying stinks, at least in my opinion. The Bible calls it a "sting," "a valley."[13] However, we don't have to let it rob us of our joy today. When we embrace our no-lose situation like Paul did, we can say with joy-filled confidence, "for to me, to live is Christ and to die is gain" (Philippians 1:21).

> BE SURE TO CARRY YOUR JOY CUBE WITH YOU ALL DAY AND PRACTICE RECITING YOUR FIRST MEMORY VERSE: PHILIPPIANS 1:21.

# TAKE THE HIGH ROAD WITHOUT FEAR

*Whatever happens, conduct yourselves in a manner worthy of the gospel of Christ. Then, whether I come and see you or only hear about you in my absence, I will know that you stand firm in the one Spirit, striving together as one for the faith of the gospel without being frightened in any way by those who oppose you. This is a sign to them that they will be destroyed, but that you will be saved—and that by God. For it has been granted to you on behalf of Christ not only to believe in him, but also to suffer for him, since you are going through the same struggle you saw I had, and now hear that I still have.*

**–PHILIPPIANS 1:27-30**

We all experience people who oppose us, challenge us, strike us, betray us, undermine us, ridicule us, or aggravate us. These individuals create circumstances and even seasons in our lives that can rob us of our joy. No joke! As a follower of Jesus, how are we to respond? The fifth axiom Paul presented to us in these verses not only instructs us on how to respond but on how this response can actually increase our joy. Let's see what Paul had to say.

In the Greek language, verses 27–30 is one long run-on sentence. My high school English teacher would have had a fit. My response: take it up with the Holy Spirit who inspired Paul to write these life-changing words. This grammatically challenging sentence contains only one directive verb: *conduct*. The word is *polis* in the Greek. It is where we get our word *politics*. Politics in Paul's day didn't have the negative connotation it has today. It wasn't about elephants and donkeys at all. It referred to the set of activities associated with making decisions in groups, or how a particular group of citizens chose to "conduct" themselves. Later in the letter Paul referred to believers in Jesus as "citizens of heaven" (3:20 NLT).

As citizens of heaven, we are called to live by the "politics," or the standards, of our homeland, even when we are living on foreign soil. You may remember these lyrics to an old song, "This world is not my home, I'm just a passin' through. My treasures are laid up somewhere beyond the blue. . . ."[1] This means we govern our life by the code of conduct from our ultimate home, heaven, laid out in our constitution, the Bible. We are called to live distinctively different lives, to stand up and to stand out for our beliefs. We are called to take the high road, regardless of what everyone else is doing.

Paul went on to say, "Then, whether I come and see you or only hear about you in my absence, I will know that you stand firm in the one Spirit, striving together as one for the faith of the gospel" (v. 27). The words *striving together* are a compound word, *sunaltheo*, in the Greek. *Sun* means "with"; *altheo* is where we get our English word *athlete*. When you put the two together, it carries the idea of athletes working together to win the race. If you have ever been on an athletic team, you know there are few things that bring more excitement in life than the experience of a team working together toward victory.

We are to do this "without being frightened in any way by those who oppose you" (v. 28). This is the only time this particular word for "frightened" is used in the New Testament. It was connected to the image of a horse shying away from battle. I have always wondered if the horse was frightened as his rider was leading him or her into a sea of opponents with swords and guns in their hands. It turns out they did get frightened and often tried to communicate this to their master by pulling away. I would be that horse.

What was Paul inviting us to do when people oppose or attack us? He called us to take the high road without fear. Followers of Jesus do not stoop to the tactics of others who are seeking to hurt us. As we grow in Christ, we do not have it in our heart to retaliate. Jesus invites us to "turn the other cheek" when someone insults us or strikes a blow to our pride or projects (Matthew 5:39). It doesn't mean we don't respond. It just means we don't respond in the same way as others. We are better than that.

We are also called not to live in fear. This is easier said than done. But the Bible tells us to "fear not" more than 365 times.[2] That is one time for every day of the year. Why? Because it is something we need to remind ourselves of every single day. Fear robs us of joy like few things can. It causes our stomachs to churn; it preoccupies our minds so we are not present with people; it keeps us awake at night, ruminating on worst-case scenarios; it leaves us terrified that our opponents will overcome us; it leads us to believe this might be how our story ends. However, when we can push aside our fears and enter the battle with confidence using a Christ-centered response, we not only honor God, the ruler of the heavenly kingdom cited on our passports, we also increase our joy. How? When we rise above our fears and let our confidence in the power of Christ reign in us, all the negative emotions I mentioned fade. Remember, we cannot remove the negative circumstances that come our way. We can and should try to dodge the unnecessary ones, but the only effective strategy is to learn to rise above them. In Christ, Paul said, this is possible.

Now look at what Paul said next. I didn't see this coming. "This is a sign to them that they will be destroyed, but that you will be saved—and that by God" (v. 28). When we don't fall apart from criticism, betrayal, and attacks, whether by people or circumstances, it sends an eerie sensation to our perpetrators' psyches that they are on the wrong side of this transaction. God has instilled in every person a sense of right or wrong (Romans 2:15). When we return nastiness with love, it pricks their conscience.

Here is even better news! If we can avoid shying away from the battle like a frightened horse and instead enter the fray with a Jesus-centered response, it confirms for us that we are saved. Why? Before God took control of our lives, we would have either been crushed by the attack or entered the battle with a vengeful hatred like our attacker. This new, unexpected response could only mean one thing: we do in fact belong to God, who is living in us. To have confirmation in your soul that you are a child of God will give a big boost to your joy levels.

Paul wrapped up this paragraph with an important message:

> For it has been granted to you on behalf of Christ not only to believe in him, but also to suffer for him, since you are going through the same struggle you saw I had, and now hear that I still have. (vv. 29–30)

He was saying that believing and suffering were given to us as a gift, a privilege. Wow, that is a hard concept to wrap our heads around! I certainly see how believing is a gift, but suffering? This is a foreign concept to our comfort-driven culture today. I am not pointing fingers. I am a comfort junkie myself. But Paul is not the only one who experienced this gift. Prior to Paul's conversion, Peter and some other disciples were being persecuted and imprisoned for their faith by the Jewish religious leaders called the Sanhedrin. After they were flogged (whipped on their bare backs) and released, this was their response: "The apostles left the Sanhedrin, *rejoicing* because they had been counted worthy of suffering disgrace for the Name" (Acts 5:41, emphasis added). Truthfully, I think this is something we need to experience to fully understand.

Bottom line, every time we choose to take the high road without fear, it increases our joy!

## DRIVING OUT FEAR

Fear robs us of joy. Agreed? But the Bible tells us that "perfect love drives out fear" (1 John 4:18). How does this work?

Neuroscientists now know that God wired our brains so that fear is our initial and fastest response to everything that comes to our five senses. As mentioned earlier, this divinely designed system is like a simple circuit board living in the basement of our brain, controlled by the amygdala. The amygdala forms the core of the neural system for processing fearful situations, as well as the appropriate fear-related behavioral response.[3]

This is a good thing when we need to quickly react to a pile of falling rocks directly above us or when we need to run from a stampede of wildebeest. We don't need to overthink it; we just need to move. However, if we are not careful, we can draw on this fear system as our default mechanism for every circumstance we face. Some people live in the basement of their brains in a chronic state of fear. (I know, I have been there.)

When someone truly opposes and attacks us, we go into fear mode and can choose "flight" (like the frightened horse mentioned by Paul) or "fight" (swinging back with our fists or words). But the Scriptures and modern science tell us there is a third way: love!

Remember the prefrontal cortex? It is bigger than the lower part of our brain, the fear center, and much more powerful. It is where the virtue and ability to love reside. When we choose to take the high road and offer love, compassion, forgiveness, prayer, and service in the place of retreat or retaliation, we overcome our fear.

Brain experts have told us it is impossible to love and fear at the same time. It is how God made us. Paul's volitional decision to walk in a worthy manner in the face of his opposition, through the power of the Holy Spirit within him, reduced his fear.

Paul recommended a second way to increase the depth of joy in our lives. When we resist fear and instead take the high road, we choose growth, which leads to greater joy. You've probably heard of post-traumatic stress disorder, but have you heard of post-traumatic growth? Oftentimes, when we've experienced traumatic events, such as going to war, bereavement, bone marrow transplantation, breast cancer, chronic illness, heart attack, natural disaster, physical assault, or refugee displacement, we struggle emotionally and mentally. But researchers have found that, while these experiences can be very difficult to manage, they also "spur profound positive growth."[4] Psychologists have coined this experience "post-traumatic growth." I love that!

Of course, post-traumatic growth is not the outcome everyone experiences. So, what distinguishes those who get stuck in the nasty cycle of their trauma from those who not only find freedom but advancement? At the very core of it all is one's mindset. This is what Paul was getting at when he invited us to take the high road without fear. This mindset changes how we perceive the cards we are dealt. It leads to a positive reinterpretation of the situation, and acceptance and focus on the problem head-on rather than avoidance or denial.

People who are ultimately successful are the ones who won't allow their circumstances to chart their course. They face challenges directly, knowing that challenges are an inevitable part of life in a broken world. They even believe these challenges will make them stronger. I like to say that these kinds of people have a B+ spiritual blood type.

## MERCY THAT TRANSFORMS

*Les Misérables*, a novel by Victor Hugo turned into a musical for the stage and big screen, provides a powerful example of taking the high road without fear to find joy.

The story opens with the main character, Jean Valjean, being released from prison after serving a nineteen-year sentence for stealing bread for his starving sister and her family and for trying to escape several times. Upon his release, he tries numerous times to stay at the local inns but is turned away because his yellow passport marks him as a former convict. This leaves him homeless, sleeping on the streets.

Out of benevolence, the local bishop gives him shelter. That night, when the bishop and his wife are asleep, Valjean runs off with the bishop's silverware. When the police capture him, they bring him back to the bishop to identify him and make their case against Valjean. However, in that moment, the bishop takes the high road and pulls out matching silver candlesticks and hands them to Valjean, telling him he forgot to take these as well, giving the impression that everything, the silverware and the candlesticks, were given as a gift. The police accept his explanation and leave. In the musical, the bishop sings these words quietly in the ear of Jean Valjean:

But remember this, my brother
See in this some higher plan
You must use this precious silver
To become an honest man
By the witness of the martyrs
By the Passion and the Blood
God has raised you out of darkness
I have saved your soul for God.[5]

Valjean is initially haunted by the grace and the calling bestowed upon him. But he ultimately resolves to give himself to this divine higher plan, and for the rest of the story he takes the high road to help people. The bishop's mercy leads to his transformation.

The villain in the story is the police inspector Javert. Once a guard in the prison where Valjean was originally held, he is a legalist who has it out for our main character. No matter how much good Jean Valjean has done in his life, Javert just can't let go of the fact that, in his own mind, Valjean belongs back in prison. Throughout the story, he pursues the ex-convict turned philanthropist with a vengeance that no doubt creates fear for Valjean.

Toward the end of the story, Valjean has an opportunity to kill Javert. This would solve all his problems. But Valjean takes the high road and lets him go. He tells Javert that he will turn himself in but asks for some time to visit his home to say goodbye. Javert agrees and tells him he will wait for him in the street, but when Valjean returns, he finds that Javert is gone.

What happened to Javert? He was caught between his strict belief in the law and the mercy Valjean showered upon him. Unable to cope with this dilemma, Javert throws himself into the Seine River.

At the end of this powerful story, Jean Valjean has led a hard life filled with horrible circumstances, but Victor Hugo tells us he died a content man. We can do the same. Like Valjean discovered, our joy is not dependent on our circumstances but on how we respond to them. If we can have faith to take the high road in our life without fear, trusting that Christ will take care of us, we will live life with a greater sense of dignity and purpose. We will live life with less regrets. Plainly put, living a principled life driven by the calling of Christ leads to a deep well of joy.

## THE JOY CHALLENGE

One of the key strategies for turning your trauma into a growth opportunity that leads to increased joy is facing the problem head-on. It's not always a choice that comes naturally. But let's learn a lesson from the buffalo.

Did you know that when a storm comes, buffalo run toward the storm? It's true. By running straight into the storm, they minimize the amount of time they experience pain. Cows, on the other hand, run away from the storm, trying to avoid it. Guess what? Cows are slow, and the storm quickly catches up with them. Because they are running in the same direction as the storm, they are in the storm a lot longer than the buffalo.

Paul was a buffalo, not a cow. And he called us to also be buffalo rather than "cow-ards" (sorry for that, couldn't help myself). Here is your Joy Challenge for today: look for an opportunity to take the high road. Follow these steps:

1. Identify a circumstance and/or a person who is opposing you right now. Write the specifics out in your journal. If you can't think of anything or anyone at the moment, be on the lookout for a challenging situation today. It can be as simple as

someone who cuts you off on the road or a negative comment you receive from a family member, friend, or coworker.

2. Think about how you can take the high road in this situation. Write down your ideas.

3. Activate your plan and write down your thoughts about the experience at the end of the day.

> REMEMBER TO CARRY YOUR JOY CUBE WITH YOU TODAY AND SHARE YOUR FIRST MEMORY VERSE (PHILIPPIANS 1:21) WITH AT LEAST ONE PERSON TODAY.

# PART 2

# JOY DESPITE PEOPLE

## MEMORY VERSES

*Therefore if you have any encouragement from being united
with Christ, if any comfort from his love, if any common
sharing in the Spirit, if any tenderness and compassion,
then make my joy complete by being like-minded, having the same love, being one in spirit and of one mind.*

### –PHILIPPIANS 2:1-2

During my freshman year of college in Springfield, Missouri, my
roommate asked me to go spelunking with him. Never heard
of it? Neither had I. The word is derived from the Latin for "cave."
Spelunking is recreational caving. Sounded like loads of fun to me,
so I said yes.

My roommate had heard of a cave that you entered on the side
of a hill next to a river. Turns out, the opening into the cave was very
small. To enter, you had to lie on your stomach and scoot yourself in.
As you scooted, you also descended into the cave. When you were

about a body and a half in, you had to turn your head to the side to fit into the opening. After scooting for roughly twenty feet, all of a sudden you'd see the earth open up into a giant room.

The stalactite and stalagmite formations were magnificent. Bats were hanging from the ceiling with no apparent interest in us (thank goodness). We weaved and turned in and out of rooms, marking our spots along the way so we knew how to exit. I was having a grand ol' time.

About twenty minutes into our adventure, the flashlight my roommate was holding went out. Please don't judge me, but it was the only flashlight we brought. It was the darkest dark I had ever experienced. To make matters worse, I couldn't find my roommate. He had been about fifteen feet away from me when the flashlight went out. When I called out to him, he didn't answer. I assumed he'd hit his head on a stalactite or something and gotten knocked out. I was terrified.

I crawled around the cave with my hands out, trying to find my roommate and the flashlight, but to no avail. I did this for ten minutes or so, but it felt like hours. Finally, I sat down and considered all my options. There were none. To make matters worse, we hadn't told anyone where we were going, so no one would know where to look for us. This was in an era way before cell phones, so I had no way to call anyone. Even if I had a cell phone, there would have been no reception that deep in the cave. I began to sob uncontrollably.

This was the end of the rope for me. *This is how I will die*, I thought, *all alone in a dark, damp cave in the middle of Missouri. It might be years before anyone discovers our bodies*. Obviously, I made it out alive and will tell you that story in a moment, but the point I'm making is that being alone is a dreadful thing. It is not how God meant for us to live or to die.

Twenty-four years after this traumatic event in my life, a new report was released entitled *Hardwired to Connect*.[1] The report revealed brain research that proves that God hardwired us to connect to people in order to lead meaningful lives. Allan Schore of UCLA's School of Medicine put it this way: "The idea is that we are born to form attachments, that our brains are physically wired to develop in tandem with another's through emotional communication beginning before words are spoken."[2]

Evolutionary psychologists have proven that our desire to form relational bonds has been hardwired in our brains from day one.[3] When we truly connect with another person, oxytocin is released in our system. Remember, oxytocin is a pleasure hormone that not only works to reduce our stress but also boosts all kinds of other positive effects in us, like improved concentration and the strengthening of our immune system. And these benefits only increase as we populate our lives with positive relationships.

In a nutshell, God's Word and modern science both conclude that we experience the greatest amount of health and happiness when we are deeply connected to God and to one another. This is why peace between us and others is so valuable.

The virtue of peace is the cousin of joy. In the New Testament, it is the word *eirēnē*. *Eirēnē* finds its meaning and roots in the Old Testament Hebrew word *shalom*. Shalom is all about peace in our relationships as the priority. When this is achieved, it is often accompanied by the feeling of peace. Dr. Larry Richards wrote, "In every theologically significant use [of the word *eirēnē*] 'peace' is something rooted in one's relationship with God and testifies to the restoration of human beings to inner harmony and to harmonious relationships with others."[4]

When things are right with God and others, our anxiety lowers and our feeling of peace rises. That is why Paul urged us in his letter to the Romans with these words: "If it is possible, as far as it depends on you, live at peace with everyone" (12:18). When things are not right in our relationship with God and others, our lives get tense and complicated. Much like how I was feeling all alone in the dark of that cave.

Back to how I made it out alive: When I began to sob, lamenting that my life was over, my roommate turned on his flashlight. Turns out, he was playing a prank on me. Needless to say, we did not room together the following year.

See if you agree with me on this. People have an uncanny ability, either intentionally or unintentionally, to suck the joy out of our lives. And the more we know a person, the more knowledgeable they are on the particular buttons to push to create the greatest agitation.

Paul had people like the Philippians who brought him great joy, but he also had people who were highly gifted at draining his pool of peace. Paul's aim in this chapter was not to tell us how to completely avoid these people, because it can't be done. You would have to become a hermit living life alone in a cave, only to discover that excessive solitary confinement will equally steal your joy. Instead, Paul's goal was to show us how to have inner joy despite these people. Anybody interested?

In the pages that follow, we will look at five new principles that will help us rise above the complexities of our relationships and guide us to a place of sustainable peace. Paul's strategy was not a defensive one but an offensive one. He taught us how we need to proactively approach our relationships, even when others are not behaving. When these principles become habitual in our lives, they will defuse the sparks before they become a wildfire.

But before we dive into our one-on-one life coaching session with the apostle Paul, let's take some time to reflect. Write your thoughts in response to the following questions in your journal:

- Which of your relationships create the greatest amount of tension for you? Can you identify the source of the tension? Is there a recurring theme?

- If the people you identified above were asked what you do to contribute to the tension, what do you think they would say?

Here is a free piece of advice I will offer apart from what Paul said. If you have a friend who invites you to go spelunking with a single flashlight, tell them no. If you decide to go and that friend plays a prank on you by turning off the flashlight in the dark recesses of the cave, well, time to find a new friend. At least that would be my first thought. But Paul offered us the opportunity to take another path that doesn't allow the actions of others to rob us of our joy. Truth is, my old roommate and I remained friends during our college years, though we never went spelunking together again. Like many relationships, we drifted apart after college but recently reunited some forty years later. Today, I don't cry about the incident—I laugh.

> BE SURE TO CARRY YOUR JOY CUBE WITH YOU ALL DAY AND START MEMORIZING PHILIPPIANS 2:1-2.

# GET ON THE SAME PAGE WITH YOUR COMMUNITY

*Therefore if you have any encouragement from being united with Christ, if any comfort from his love, if any common sharing in the Spirit, if any tenderness and compassion, then make my joy complete by being like-minded, having the same love, being one in spirit and of one mind.*

**–PHILIPPIANS 2:1-2**

Sixteenth-century Dutch philosopher Desiderius Erasmus once declared, "Women, you can't live with them, you can't live without them."[1] I am pretty sure this statement applies to both men and women (and all the women said, "Amen!"). We need one another, but we needle one another. One famous comic strip of our day put it this way: "I love mankind, it's people I can't stand."[2]

Paul no doubt wrestled with this same sentiment. We discovered in chapter 1 of Philippians that people were trying to take over the platform of his ministry while he was quarantined under house arrest. It might've been like someone moving in to take over your job while you are out on maternity leave or recovering from surgery. Paul was also wrestling with false teachers who were entering the church at Philippi and drawing people away from the true gospel of grace (3:1–3). Then, there was the inward squabbling of two ladies in the church that Paul needed to confront (4:1–3). Whether you lived in the first century or live in the twenty-first century, some things never change, particularly among family members, whether biological or spiritual. We've got to find a way to not let this human condition take away our joy.

Paul began this passage by pleading with the Philippian believers based on the benefits their faith in Jesus had afforded them. He used the classic if-then formula. "If you have received this benefit, and you most certainly have, then honor my request." Paul invited them to consider the encouragement, the comfort, the fellowship, the tenderness, and the compassion they had received from being united with and loved by Christ. Their relationship with Jesus had given them the hope of eternal life and victory over death. They were part of a new family tree of faith called to a new level of love and virtue. A relationship with Jesus had put them in a no-lose situation with a life filled with purpose.

The benefits were overwhelming and obvious, but Paul wanted them to acknowledge it for themselves. He wanted their hearts to overflow with gratitude. As fellow Christians, we need to do the same thing. We don't bow down to the principles of the Bible because we must, but because we can't help ourselves. The grace we have received in Christ, the new family we have been adopted into, and the comfort and compassion that have helped us through difficult and dark seasons of life should motivate us to live differently than before.

Here is the "then" to Paul's "if" statements: If you are nodding your head in agreement (and you should be), then "make my joy complete" (v. 2). There is that word again: *joy*. If the believers in Philippi did what Paul asked of them, it would take Paul's joy level to a place of completion. The image is of a cup of your favorite beverage being filled to the brim.

So, what was he asking of them? He was asking them to get on the same page with one another. Paul defined his ask with four requests:

- Think alike
- Love alike
- Be of one soul
- Be of one mind

Here is a saying that I think aptly summarizes what Paul was getting at:

> In the essentials, unity.
> In the nonessentials, liberty.
> In all things, charity.

We don't know who wrote these wonderful words. I wish I could take credit for them, because it gives us a lovely rubric from which we can engage our relationships successfully. Dr. F. F. Bruce put it this way:

> This is not a matter of making everyone see eye-to-eye or have the same opinion on every subject. Life would be very flat and dull without the give-and-take practiced when a variety of opinions and viewpoints provide scope for friendly discussion and debate.[3]

The secret, then, for every family and every spiritual community is to define the handful of essential things we all embrace. We should think alike on such things as:

- Truthfulness: We speak the truth to one another.
- Promises: We keep the promises we make to one another.
- Respect: We respect one another.
- Addiction: We don't allow addictions to overtake our lives.

When it comes to matters like these, we are all on the same page, of one mind. Most everything else becomes nonessential. Things like:

- Money management
- Food choices
- Political views
- Exercise routines
- Driving styles
- Cold oranges or room-temperature oranges
- Toilet paper—over or under?
- Piercings and tattoos (once you are eighteen)
- Ford or Chevy or neither
- How to raise and discipline children
- Rock and roll or classical music

Certainly, you have your own opinion and conviction on these topics, but you let others take a different approach. You grant them the liberty to choose their own path and preferences. This is a sign of maturity that very few people reach, because it is hard to give up the desire to be right about everything.

And here is the final challenge. Even if someone violates the essentials or embraces a different belief system, you love them. "In all things, charity." This is the supreme call of Christians, as modeled by Jesus himself. Paul said to the Philippian believers, "If you can take on this attitude and approach to life, it will make my joy complete." Truthfully, it wouldn't just make Paul's joy complete; it would make their own joy complete.

## THE POWER OF ONENESS

Once again modern science on the brain gives us insight as to why Paul's principles work to increase our joy. Neuro-theologian Dr. Jim Wilder wrote,

> We do not directly choose to be joyful any more than we can choose to have low blood pressure. The joy and blood pressure systems in the brain are not subject to direct choice. Joy levels are regulated indirectly through relationships. Increasing joy will involve improving our relational skill, training our brain, and getting involved in tightly bonded community.[4]

We nourish that kind of tightly bonded community Wilder mentioned when we are "one in spirit," as Paul put it. "One in spirit" is better translated as "with one soul." We think of our souls as being inside of us as individuals, but we can move with our brothers and sisters in Christ in unity, as "one in spirit." When a family or a church community are on the same page, living in harmony as one soul, everybody's joy meter spikes. But when a family or community are not on the same page, the opposite happens.

I didn't grow up in a Christian home. My parents were not followers of Jesus. To top it off, my dad was one of eleven children raised by a single parent, my grandmother. He never had a healthy model for what a good husband and father looked like. As a result of my dad's immaturity, my parents were often not on the same page, and it created great tension in our home.

I remember my parents having screaming matches at night while we were in bed trying to sleep. I shared a bedroom with my older brother and younger sister, and we would look at one another with terror on our faces. I would then take my pillow and cover my ears with it. Over the years, I watched my brother, who was five years older than me, shift from terror to anger. There were times that my dad would give my mom the silent treatment for weeks on end, wouldn't talk to her at all. We walked around the house like there were eggshells on the ground. This is not the environment God intended little boys and girls to experience.

I can't even begin to tell you how this bruised and crushed my spirit as a little boy. I felt tension in my stomach and anxiety swarming in my head. I felt insecure and vulnerable. It most definitely robbed me of joy. I remember reading that the number one thing a child wants from his parents is to know they are undeniably in love with each other. I totally agree. I carried these wounds well into my adult years, and it affected my relationship with other people, especially my wife.

When there is tension in the home or in the church community, it robs everyone of joy, not just the people in conflict with one another. We are called to something more. Christians are to live distinctively different lives for the sake of others, to live in charity and love. We have the responsibility to promote unity and harmony in our relationships to do our part in creating environments of joy. I love the brutal honesty Dr. Daniel Amen offered on this subject. He wrote,

> We all have the capacity to control how we express ourselves, no matter how we feel. I can prove it. Imagine someone who is just acting miserably to his or her spouse when somebody comes to the

door. Have you ever noticed how nicely such a person will treat the stranger? How were they able—in a split second—to go from inflicting their awful mood on their spouse to acting beautifully toward the stranger who's at the door? Obviously, we can control our moods.[5]

This is precisely what Paul called us to practice today. If we will practice harmony and cultivate oneness with the people in our lives, in concert with the other principles he presented, our joy will be complete. And we will be doing our part to create an environment where the people around us are set up to do the same.

## THE JOY CHALLENGE

So here is your challenge for this joy principle. Psychologists call it *positive reinforcement*. Basically, you proactively notice what you like about others more than what you don't like. The goal is to spot and call out five positive things for every one negative thing in another person.

Research shows that married couples who put this challenge into practice are significantly less likely to get divorced.[6] This principle not only works in marriages but in business. In the same study, businesses with a higher rate of negative comments produced the lowest-performing teams.

I want you to try this out on one person today. Think about choosing a person who might dance to the beat of a different drummer than you do. Maybe they voted for a different candidate in the last election or have a bunch of tattoos or none (depending on your point of view). You may want to choose your mate, your child, your mom or dad, or your best friend—definitely someone you will be spending some time with today.

Dr. Amen encouraged us to look for micro-moments of loving behavior in the little everyday things. When you spot it, let the other person know. Get it done. Don't go over the top with your comments, but make sure to be positive. If five comments to the same person in one day seems overwhelming, feel free to do a few less. Just make sure you give that person more positive comments than negative ones. As a matter of fact, let's make today a negative-free day.

At the end of the day, write out your thoughts in your journal.

CARRY YOUR JOY CUBE WITH YOU ALL DAY AND CONTINUE MEMORIZING PHILIPPIANS 2:1–2, AS WELL AS REHEARSING YOUR FIRST MEMORY VERSE (PHILIPPIANS 1:21).

# ELEVATE OTHERS ABOVE YOURSELF

*Do nothing out of selfish ambition or vain conceit. Rather, in humility value others above yourselves, not looking to your own interests but each of you to the interests of the others. In your relationships with one another, have the same mindset as Christ Jesus:*

*Who, being in very nature God,*
 *did not consider equality with God something to be*
  *used to his own advantage;*
*rather, he made himself nothing*
 *by taking the very nature of a servant,*
 *being made in human likeness.*
*And being found in appearance as a man,*
 *he humbled himself*
 *by becoming obedient to death—*
  *even death on a cross!*

*Therefore God exalted him to the highest place*
*and gave him the name that is above every name,*
*that at the name of Jesus every knee should bow,*
*in heaven and on earth and under the earth,*
*and every tongue acknowledge that Jesus Christ is Lord,*
*to the glory of God the Father.*

**-PHILIPPIANS 2:3-11**

The only pathway to achieve principle #6—Get on the Same Page with Your Community—is to embrace it in your heart and then apply it through your behavior in the upcoming principle #7: Elevate Others Above Yourself. Unity is impossible if each person is out for themselves, each promoting their own cause, each seeking their own advantage.[1]

As we discovered in our last chapter, when the quality of our relationships is up, so is the quality of our joy. God has wired all of us this way, so no one can escape this reality. We are called to do our part to maintain peace in our relationships (Romans 12:18). However, sometimes—many times—people don't do their part. We are left to decide how we will respond to the bad behavior of others. Coach Paul taught how to do that in three parts: two things to stop doing and one thing to continue doing.

## DON'T #1: "DO NOTHING OUT OF SELFISH AMBITION OR VAIN CONCEIT."

Some incorrectly read this to mean we cannot have ambition or drive in our lives. This is not what Paul was asking of us. Proper ambition is necessary for getting up every day and living out our purpose with excellence. This is a principle to increase our joy that we will discover a little later on. Paul was referring to a brand of ambition that pulls others down, an ambition that is selfish. When people spot this in a person, it is repulsive and distasteful and repels people—certainly not a way to win friends and influence people.

"Vain conceit," on the other hand, is a compound word in Greek (*keno* + *doxia*) that means "empty opinion." Dr. Hawthorne described such a person this way: "A person who is motivated by kenodoxia is a person who assertively, even arrogantly claims to have the right opinion (doxia), but who in fact is in error (kenos). He is a person who is conceited without reason; deluded."[2] This is someone who thinks they are right about every subject, when in fact they are not. It is a person who will fight you to prove his idea is right while everyone around him knows it's not. This person is usually blinded as to how they are coming across to others.

Paul invited the Philippian believers and us to consider whether we may be operating out of selfish ambition or vain conceit. I don't know about you, but I don't want to be that guy. One of the wisest words you will hear from someone is, "I don't know. What do you think?"

## DO: "IN HUMILITY VALUE OTHERS ABOVE YOURSELVES."

If we are not careful, we can easily misunderstand humility as we do selfish ambition. As C. S. Lewis put it, a really humble man "will not be thinking about humility: he will not be thinking about himself at all."[3] Read that again. This is hard to do in our world today, but it is essential if you want access to the well of pure joy. Interestingly, the word *humility* was never used as a positive virtue in Greek culture or writings until it appeared in the New Testament. In the world, humility is a weakness; in the Christian faith, it is a strength—a virtue.[4]

There are a few very important truths in our world that we need to stand up for and defend—and then there are a lot of preferences. A humble person knows the difference. Additionally, humility is not just a call to value others to whom all willingly bow, but those who lack status as well. A true sign of a person who has captured the heart of humility is one who listens intently to the opinion of another person, particularly if they consider them to be of a lowly status, or at least a lower status than them.

## DON'T #2: "NOT LOOKING TO YOUR OWN INTERESTS BUT EACH OF YOU TO THE INTEREST OF THE OTHERS."

Here the focus is not just an admonition against being self-centered but a call to proactively keep an eye out to discover the interests of others. The believer forms a habit in every relationship and in every group to ponder what might best serve the other person or group before action is taken. It is the act and privilege of laying down our right to be right or to get our way in every situation. This is spiritual maturity at another level. This is being like Jesus. How would this approach transform marriages, friendships, work relationships, and even the church?

# A QUESTION OF ESTEEM

Elevating others above yourself will increase your joy despite the actions of other people, because God chooses to favor the person who approaches life this way. He steps in and offers a hand up to the humble. We see this over and over again throughout the Bible.

- God shows favor to the humble. (Proverbs 3:34; 1 Peter 5:5)
- God lifts up and exalts the humble. (Luke 14:11; James 4:10)
- God gives grace to the humble. (James 4:6)
- God gives honor and a more satisfying life to the humble. (Proverbs 18:12, 22:4)
- God hears the prayers of the humble. (2 Chronicles 7:14)

- God gives the humble a position of greatness in the kingdom of heaven. (Matthew 18:4)

You can't beat having God on your side! And yet it can still be a struggle to choose the way of humility. Why is that? I have discovered that most people who struggle with biblical humility also struggle with low self-esteem. They have a fundamental belief that they are inferior to other people and, as a result, act out that belief in their relationships by finding ways to elevate themselves above others.

A blowhard Air Force major was promoted to colonel and got a brand-new office. His first morning behind the desk an airman knocked on the door and asked to speak to him. The colonel, feeling the urge to impress the young man, picked up his phone and said, "Yes, General, thank you. Yes, I will pass this along to the president this afternoon. Yes, goodbye, sir." Then, turning to the airman, he barked, "And what do you want?"

"Nothing important, sir. I just came to hook up your telephone."

When you come across people who struggle to elevate others above themselves, it almost always comes back to the issue of identity. They are fighting to convince themselves that they are a somebody. They are clawing for a jolt of joy that comes from sensing that they are significant. It really is a sad thing to watch. I know. I haven't just seen a lot of people living this way, but I have given it plenty of attempts in my own life, to my embarrassment. Fortunately, Paul gave us an eloquent and classy alternative.

## LAYING DOWN YOUR RIGHTS

Paul offered four stories of people who model biblical humility: Jesus (Philippians 2:5–11), Paul himself (vv. 12–18), Timothy (vv. 19–24), and Epaphroditus (vv. 25–30). Let's focus on the supreme example, Jesus.

Paul invited us to shift our mindset to match that of Jesus, and he did that by telling us about what Jesus did. The story begins in verse 6 with the truth that Jesus is God. Jesus knows who he is. His identity is unquestionable. But here's the kicker. Jesus told us that if we receive him and believe in his name, we are given the right to become children of God (John 1:12). With this right, we become full heirs of the kingdom of God (Romans 8:16–17). We no longer have to pretend we are a somebody; we already are a somebody in Christ.

In Christ, we no longer have anything to prove. Nothing anybody says or does can alter the reality of who we are in Christ. Our identity is not based on other people's assessment of us, so we don't need to give them that power over us. Our worth is based on God's assessment of us, and all he can see is that you and I are washed clean in the blood of Jesus. Biblical humility flows out of a person not with low self-esteem but with high God esteem. This frees us to focus on building others up. This is the way Christ did it.

Paul wrote, "He made himself nothing by taking the very nature of a servant. . . . He humbled himself by becoming obedient to death—even death on a cross!" (Philippians 2:7–8). What was Jesus doing? *Jesus laid down his right . . . and so should I.* The passage says Jesus "made himself nothing." It doesn't say that someone else made him nothing or pushed him down. He chose to give up his right; he laid it down voluntarily. Think about that.

The God of the universe who owns "the cattle on a thousand hills" (Psalm 50:10) decided to enter our world poor. The God who has access to all power and all knowledge restricted his knowledge and power so he could relate to us. The God of the universe washed the dirty feet of the disciples and then instructed them to do the same. The God of the universe, who did nothing wrong, took on our wrongs and died to pay for them. He invites us to put down our pride and to take up our cross and follow him in this same kind of sacrificial life.

The Bible says that pride, or the lack of humility, brings whole nations down. It's a big deal. But it also brings families and friendships down every day. And the lack of humility raises its ugly head in the smallest of ways. We can see examples of this in all kinds of relationships, but perhaps especially in marriage.

Rozanne, my wife, likes to back her car into the garage. I always thought it was a colossal waste of time. But did I want to be right (which I was sure I was), or did I want to lay it down to value her wishes over mine? Recently, I was introduced to research that shows that successful people actually do back their cars into the garage.[5] Ouch. Turns out I was the one struggling with vain conceit—being conceited without reason, deluded.

But sometimes I do get it right. The other day Rozanne and I were in a conversation with a group of people and I mentioned how long Rozanne and I have been married. She corrected me right in front of the group. Well, guess what? I was right, and she was wrong! The question swirled around in my mind: *Do I correct her, or do I let it go?* Frankly, I despise couples who correct each other in public. I think it is one of the reasons young people are not getting married today. But should I have taken advantage of this rare opportunity where I knew I was right, or should I have, instead, let it go? On that occasion, I let it go. Later, when we were alone, Rozanne recognized she was wrong and asked why I hadn't corrected her. I said, "Because you mean more to me than being right on a fact that doesn't really matter. What matters is that you still want to be married to me." Okay, folks, how do you think that played out for me? We had a house filled with joy that evening!

The issues that present themselves in our relationships every day can be teeny tiny, but how we respond says a whole lot about what we think about the other person. Christ laid down his life and died for Rozanne. Can I follow him and consider her needs above my own? Can I at least back her car into the garage?

Christians do not need to claw and fight and boast to get our way. We are called to walk humbly before the Lord and esteem others above ourselves. In time, God will exalt us. Jesus said, "For those who exalt themselves will be humbled, and those who humble themselves will be exalted" (Matthew 23:12). Trust him, and find rest and joy for your souls.

## THE JOY CHALLENGE

I was recently on vacation with some lovely new friends. I spent time asking about their upbringing, work, and hobbies, and the more I probed, the more interesting stories came out. Everybody has a story worth listening to. I find a real story is better than a made-up one on television. It is interesting, however, that during the four days I was with these new people, they never once asked anything about *my* story. This is, unfortunately, something that happens often in conversation, even if people do not mean to do it. When we are not mindful, we can get caught up so much in ourselves that we lose focus on others. So let's practice that today.

Here is the first of two challenges for you today. Go through the whole day without talking about yourself or your situation. Rather, spend the whole day asking people about their day and their story—all day. Believe me, it is tougher than it sounds.

Challenge two for today: Find at least two occasions to say out loud, "I don't know . . . what do you think?" If you know someone has just read a book about the rain forest in the Amazon, say to them, "I don't know much about that. Can you tell me what you learned?"

If you are in a discussion on the state of the economy and you are not the secretary of the Treasury Department, hold back and say, "I really don't know, but I would love to hear what you think." Find someone at school or at work or in your neighborhood and say, "I don't know much about where you grew up or about your family. Do you mind sharing that with me?" Be mindful not to switch to your story in the middle of the conversation, but keep probing them on their story.

At the end of the day, write about your experiences in your journal.

CARRY YOUR JOY CUBE WITH YOU ALL DAY AND CONTINUE MEMORIZING PHILIPPIANS 2:1–2, AS WELL AS REHEARSING YOUR FIRST MEMORY VERSE (PHILIPPIANS 1:21).

# STOP BEING A GRUMP

*Therefore, my dear friends, as you have always obeyed—not only in my presence, but now much more in my absence—continue to work out your salvation with fear and trembling, for it is God who works in you to will and to act in order to fulfill his good purpose.*

*Do everything without grumbling or arguing, so that you may become blameless and pure, "children of God without fault in a warped and crooked generation." Then you will shine among them like stars in the sky as you hold firmly to the word of life. And then I will be able to boast on the day of Christ that I did not run or labor in vain. But even if I am being poured out like a drink offering on the sacrifice and service coming from your faith, I am glad and rejoice with all of you. So you too should be glad and rejoice with me.*

**–PHILIPPIANS 2:12-18**

Paul used the words *glad* and *rejoice* a total of four times at the end of our Scripture passage. What was the cause of his gladness and joy and for his invitation for us to join in with him? It has everything to do with not being a grumpy person.

Leading up to our next Joy Challenge, Paul told us we can do it. We can grow day by day to be more like Christ. He admonished us to "work out your own salvation." Keep in mind, he is not asking us to "work for" our salvation but rather to "work out" our salvation. Yes, our salvation was paid for in full by Christ's sacrifice on the cross, so we don't have to earn it. But salvation is also not only positional but experiential and should be realized in the daily life of the believer. Working it out means that we grow up into our new identity as children of God who will inherit eternal life in the kingdom of God and set our sights on looking and living more like Jesus every day.

Paul told us that we are not left to work it out on our own. God is at work *in* us to help us work it *out* of us. The word *work* in the Greek is where we get our word *energy*. God empowers and fuels us on the inside to undergo this transformation and then act it out in our day-to-day lives with other people.

What does the divine momentum of God enable us to do? To not be grumpy people. What does that mean? Paul said, "Do everything without grumbling or arguing" (v. 14). *Grumbling* in the Greek is *gaggūsō*. Try to say that out loud. The word mimics the act of grumbling, doesn't it? It refers to words spoken behind another's back. It is a murmuring or secret talk or whispering about someone where you issue a complaint or displeasure concerning another human being. It is a form of gossip, a betrayal.

Very few things hurt as much as the betrayal of a friend or co-worker. Of the nine circles of hell in Dante's *Inferno*, those guilty of betrayal are not only in the final circle, the deepest part of hell filled with people frozen in an icy lake, but they are considered to have committed the very worst offense and thus are punished in the inner depth of eternal suffering. The character representing this place is Judas, who sold out Jesus for thirty pieces of silver.

This is what we are doing when we engage in the act of *gaggūsō*. It is so easy to get caught up in it, and yet it is so devasting to the intended recipient when they find out—and they often do. It destroys unity and trust and creates tension in our relationships, families, churches, and organizations that rob us of joy—even the culprit gets bitten in the end. Paul said, in every situation you find yourself in, don't do this.

The second thing Paul said not to do is argue. The Greek word Paul used here is *dialogismos*, where we get our English word *dialogue*. But this is no benign conversation he was referring to. These dialogues are filled with strife and hurtful words that tear families and churches apart. "Sticks and stones may break my bones, but words will never hurt me"? Not these words. They sting; they leave a scar. We should not be known as a person who turns every conversation into an argument and leaves behind a string of scarred people.

Paul was in no way suggesting that we should never engage in spirited conversations on important issues or that we should all think alike. Rather, he was challenging our approach. We should never grumble or attack another person behind their back. If you have a grievance, tell them respectfully to their face. If you don't have the courage to do this or don't feel the timing is right, then keep your mouth shut. Don't scurry off to another person to share a piece of your mind.

Why do we work so hard to evade these two relational pitfalls? Paul wanted us to avoid acting this way toward one another "so that you may become blameless and pure, 'children of God without fault in a warped and crooked generation.'" The word *pure* here means "to mix, to mingle." For the people reading this letter, it would have brought up the image of "undiluted wine."[1] Our speech should taste like a full-bodied glass of Cabernet Sauvignon from Napa Valley. It is not watered down but pure and authentic.

He also calls us "children of God." Our speech, body language, and attitude should bear a family resemblance—in this case, a resemblance to God himself. Paul was essentially calling us to live up to our identity as members of the family of God, because this is who we are (1 John 3:1). When we do this, we will "shine . . . like stars" (Philippians 2:15). We become like the Star of David that led the wise men to Jesus. When our life and speech match the "word of life," we point people to a better way of life, life in Christ.

Paul wrapped up by telling the Philippian believers that when they chose to live this way, energized by the power of God within them, it brought him joy. When we are grumpy, we bring people down. We snag their joy away from them. When we live like Jesus, it lifts the spirits of everyone within striking distance of our presence, including ourselves. Paul invited the Philippian church and us to join him in this constellation of gladness.

## THE NEGATIVITY TRAP

Unfortunately, we seem to be pretty far from living the joyful lives Paul called us to live. It's easy for us to fall into the negativity trap, isn't it? Believe me, I am not pointing fingers. If left unchecked, I get stuck there often.

That is why Paul, in his letter to the Corinthians (who really struggled with their attitude), challenged them to "take captive every thought and make it obedient to Christ" (2 Corinthians 10:5). I love this image. Instead of letting thoughts enter the territory of our brains without any restrictions, we capture them and hold them for questioning. Before the thought is released, it must conform to the way of Jesus. Communication pathologist and neuroscientist Dr. Caroline Leaf says that by capturing "these rogue thoughts, you in effect direct your attention to stop the negative impact and rewire healthy new circuits in your brain."[2]

When we perceive something as negative or a threat to us, it signals our brain to get grumpy, to gear up for some grumbling and some arguing. That sucks the life out of us and everyone in the room. It also wreaks havoc on our insides. Dr. Leaf wrote,

> Not catching and stopping those thoughts leads to negative, toxic thoughts being wired into our brain; this can lead to depressive thoughts, which causes the body to go into stage two of stress. In response, the immune system produces proteins called *cytokines*, including one called *Interleukin-6*, as a positive, inflammatory response to protect the brain and body against stress. If the stress is not controlled, the depression increases, and the person moves into stage 3; over time the inflammation also increases and can lead to arteriosclerosis (hardening of the arteries) and cardiovascular disease.[3]

I'm not sure what all that means but it doesn't sound promising. That is why Paul's admonition for us in these verses is so important. He was calling us to a new standard. He was inviting us to a better place—a place where we lift one another up versus tearing one another down, a place where there isn't strife but peace and even a touch of tranquility that calms our hearts and lowers our blood pressure. As Paul said, a place of rejoicing. Count me in!

## JUST A GRUMPY OLD MAN

Back in the mid-'90s, I was a young husband, a father of four, and a pastor not making much money. We owned an older but charming home on a street that used to be a pecan-tree orchard. We didn't have much, but we made things work and we were quite grateful.

I did have one particular struggle. We didn't have an in-ground sprinkler system. For hours every week, I had to move a little sprinkler all over the front and back yards. Nobody's got time for that, particularly a young pastor of a growing church with four small children. We didn't have the money to hire someone to install a system, so one of my associate pastors joined me to install it ourselves. Neither one of us had done this before, and this was before DIY YouTube videos. What could possibly go wrong? Answer? Absolutely nothing. We installed the system without a hitch, and in two days we fired it up. The sprinklers were timed to go off at 4:00 a.m. on select days and were finished running before I even got up. I love it when a plan comes together.

A few days later, I was out in the backyard working when I heard my next-door neighbor. I peered over the wooden privacy fence between us like a scene out of the old sitcom *Home Improvement* and said, "Howdy, neighbor."

Alex was an older British gentleman with a proper English accent. Then it happened. He laid into me with words that can't be repeated in a Christian book, but here is the essence of the message: "Do you know your sprinklers are shooting water over the fence into my property and soaking my wood-shingle roof?! You and your buddy who helped you install the system are idiots. You need to fix this right away, or you are going to have legal troubles coming your way!"

Not only were my hopes of winning Yard of the Year from the Home and Garden Club dashed in a second, but I was also completely crushed. Turns out, we did install the sprinklers in the wrong location, and I needed to make it right. But did he have to approach me that way?

Fast-forward one week. Alex came knocking at our front door with a new request. I wasn't home, but my wife, Rozanne, was. There was a large tree between our houses that was on our property. Alex wanted to know if we could take it out and share the cost.

Rozanne answered in a kind and gentle voice, "Alex, I am sure Randy would be happy to work with you on this, but, truthfully, you really hurt his feelings the other day regarding the sprinklers. He doesn't want to destroy your property and is working on fixing it. In the meantime, he has turned the system off and is hand watering again. If you could have just been a little kinder in your tone. I'm not sure now is a good time to approach Randy on this new project."

Then he said it. He said, "I'm just a grumpy old man!"

But later that day, Alex did something that few people do. He owned it. When he saw me pull into the drive, he walked over and, with tears in his eyes, genuinely apologized for his words. He pulled himself out of negativity and approached me in humility. And it changed everything.

Not only did we take the tree out between our houses, but Alex helped me correctly reinstall the sprinkler system. Alex even helped me with numerous projects over the ensuing years. We became good friends.

We eventually moved out of the neighborhood and out of the state, but we would often make a point to stop by and see Alex and his wife, Eve, to share a glass of tea and catch up on life. When I heard of Alex's passing, instead of thinking, *Good riddance to a grumpy man*, I cried. I'd lost a good friend.

## THE JOY CHALLENGE

It takes vision and intentionality to stop being a grouch. You've got to own it like Alex did. If we leave our life unattended, that is exactly where we will end up, and, believe me, there is no joy at this address.

Paul laid out the vision that we would resemble our spiritual brother and Savior, Jesus. We must say to our hearts every day, "This is who I want to become."

That vision must be coupled with intentionality. We must intend to work toward our vision. From intent we must identify the means to get there. If this is your vision and you intend with God's energy working within you to get there, let me recommend our Joy Challenge for this principle, a means for not being a grumpy person.

Let's take a cue from neurosurgeon Benjamin Libet's discovery. He monitored the electrical brain activity of people who were awake while he was performing brain surgery on them (don't try this at home). He would ask them to move their finger and see how long it would take them to perform the action. Over and over again, he discovered the time between the urge to move a finger and the actual movement contained a lag of a quarter-second.[4] In other words, there is a span of time, however small, between our initial urges and our corresponding actions.

So, here is your Joy Challenge. There are going to be things coming at you all day—things you see, things you hear, things you touch, things you smell, and things you taste. It can be from watching the news, driving to work, participating in a conversation, walking into a bathroom, sitting in a meeting, taking a phone call, or even eating dinner. Information from your senses will be sent to your thalamus. At that moment, you have a quarter-second to decide either to give in to your natural tendencies toward grumpiness or to pause and evaluate what is really going on before you respond.

Today, take the most challenging situation you come across and determine that you are not going to let it bring you down. You are not going to allow it to make you grumpy or talk behind someone's back. You are not going to engage in an argument that scars others—not today. Take control of that quarter-second between urge and response.

At the end of the day, record your thoughts in your journal.

CARRY YOUR JOY CUBE WITH YOU ALL DAY AND CONTINUE MEMORIZING PHILIPPIANS 2:1–2, AS WELL AS REHEARSING YOUR FIRST MEMORY VERSE (PHILIPPIANS 1:21).

# PRINCIPLE #9

# CELEBRATE OTHER PEOPLE'S SUCCESS

*I hope in the Lord Jesus to send Timothy to you soon, that I also may be cheered when I receive news about you. I have no one else like him, who will show genuine concern for your welfare. For everyone looks out for their own interests, not those of Jesus Christ. But you know that Timothy has proved himself, because as a son with his father he has served with me in the work of the gospel. I hope, therefore, to send him as soon as I see how things go with me. And I am confident in the Lord that I myself will come soon.*

**–PHILIPPIANS 2:19-24**

Paul's explicit purpose for penning this paragraph has seemingly little to do with increasing our joy. But, as we said at the beginning of this journey, upwards of half of the twenty principles on increasing our joy are implicit. We discover them by observing how Paul was living and responding to people and things around him and what was bringing him joy as he sat in prison.

Paul laid out his intent in this passage to send his young prodigy, Timothy, to the church in Philippi. Paul's desire was to make sure they received him based on his confidence in Timothy. That is the gist of this paragraph. You will notice, however, that Paul threw the word *cheer* into the mix. Receiving good news about the Philippians would have been a boost to Paul's joy level, a pick-me-up. *The Message* translation says, "Oh, how that will do my heart good!"

What was Paul doing to increase his joy? He was celebrating other people's success.

Very few people discover this wonderful access point to joy. We get super focused on ourselves and sometimes then get a bit jealous of the success of others. But when we, instead, celebrate others and speak that to them and even broadcast it to others, it can bring us personal joy. Some might say it embarrasses them, but I promise you, when they lay their head on their pillow at night when no one is around, it proves to be a sweet experience for the recipient of your praise.

In this passage, Paul not only anticipated a successful report from the Philippians when word got back to him, but he expressed how proud he was of young Timothy and how much Timothy meant to him. Timothy had a long and intimate relationship with the church at Philippi (Acts 16:3; 17:14–15; 19:22; 20:3–4). It's not like Paul had to send his resume along with a glowing endorsement for them to accept Timothy. Second only to Paul, the Philippians loved Timothy. I think Paul was writing these wonderful things about Timothy for Timothy's sake.

Paul considered Timothy his spiritual son. We know from Paul's personal letter to Timothy that Timothy came to faith from the influence of his grandmother and mother (2 Timothy 1:5). They were Jewish. Timothy's dad was a Greek, and we are not sure what role he played in Timothy's life, at least on a spiritual front. Sons and daughters long to hear the affirmation of their fathers. Whether Timothy heard words of unconditional love and approval from his biological dad, we know he received them from Paul.

When Paul said, "I have no one else like him," he was saying they were like-minded. The Greek word is *isopsychos*. Sixteenth-century Dutch scholar Erasmus translated the verse, "I will send him as my alter ego."[1] Today we might say that Timothy was a "chip off the old block."

Then Timothy was given the highest compliment when Paul compared him to Jesus. He told the Philippians that Timothy didn't look out for his own interests but for the interests of others. This is the hallmark of the life of Jesus that Paul just addressed a few verses back. Now he was attributing it to Timothy. If someone said that about me, it would take me days to stop thinking about it.

Furthermore, the trip from Rome to Philippi was eight hundred miles. Remember, there were no planes, trains, or automobiles available. A round trip was sixteen hundred miles. It would take an estimated eighty days to make that trip. I'm not sure I would want to do it—but Timothy volunteered. What a guy! Paul celebrated the man Timothy had become and wrote it down for all to read. How do you think that made Timothy feel? It likely filled his joy bucket up pretty fast. And when Paul saw how his words, which cost him nothing, lifted the spirits of Timothy, it cheered him up as well. Celebrating others is like completing an electrical circuit. It turns the lights on in our life, it powers our motivation for living, and it gives a jolt of positive energy to our souls.

But this was not a one-and-done occurrence. Timothy was not the only one Paul celebrated. As Paul was wrapping up his letter to the Romans, he penned these words: "Everyone has heard about your obedience, so I rejoice because of you" (16:19). Paul found joy in the spiritual success of these believers as well. Young Timothy went on another trip for Paul. This time, he left from Athens, Greece, where Paul was at the time, and headed to Thessalonica, about a 410-mile trek. After hanging out with the believers and hearing their story, he brought good news back to Paul about their spiritual success. After he received the news from travel-worn Timothy, Paul sat down and penned the first of two letters to them. Listen to what Paul wrote about the believers in Thessalonica: "For what is our hope, our joy, or the crown in which we will glory in the presence of our Lord Jesus when he comes? Is it not you? Indeed, you are our glory and joy" (1 Thessalonians 2:19–20). Unable to contain himself, he came back at it again in a later chapter: "How can we thank God enough for you in return for all the joy we have in the presence of our God because of you?" (3:9). Paul found great joy in their success.

There were many days life dished out disappointment to Paul, particularly as he was quarantined in prison. Yet, on days when he wasn't experiencing many wins, he turned his attention to the success of other people. He not only internalized their success, but he also externalized it by sharing it with others through his writings. This no doubt brought joy to the recipients of his words and cheered up Paul as well.

If Paul were sitting with you and me right now, I think he would say, "You know, the same will work for you too. Why don't you give it a try?"

## RESPONDING TO OTHERS' GOOD NEWS

Research explains why what Paul suggested about celebrating others is effective in increasing our joy. Take, for example, the work of social psychologist Shelly Gable and a team of other highly qualified psychologists. Most research seems to focus on how we deal with one another when things are bad, but the aim of their studies probed the opposite question: What do you do when things go right? They wanted to look at the intrapersonal and interpersonal benefits of sharing positive events with one another.

As you might expect, sharing good news with someone, who in turn actively celebrates that news, has a profound way of increasing everyone's joy. It not only multiplies the benefits of the positive event; it strengthens the bond between the two people involved, which raises joy levels.[2]

Two years later, Dr. Gable took her research to another level by pondering the question, "Will you be there for me when things go right?" She uncovered four different types of responses people give to someone else's good news, and only one of them contributes positively to the relationship.[3]

- **ACTIVE-CONSTRUCTIVE**: Issues an enthusiastic response. Engages a conversation that allows the other person to linger and elaborate on the good news they just shared. In this style you hear comments like, "That's just terrific." "Can you give me more details of how it unfolded?" "How are you feeling right now?" This is the winning response.
- **PASSIVE-CONSTRUCTIVE**: Here we have short comments that show minimal interest in the news shared. Comments like, "Oh, that's nice." The conversation usually ends here or the topic is changed. This can be just as destructive as an outright negative response.
- **ACTIVE-DESTRUCTIVE**: Here the response pours cold water to douse the fire of the good news. In this style you might hear comments like, "I sure hope you can actually do that job."

Or, "I suppose this will mean even less time for your family." Sometimes the person making a comment like this truly believes they are being helpful.

- **PASSIVE-DESTRUCTIVE:** This is the worst response of them all. Here the person simply ignores the news altogether. They might say something like, "What are we having for dinner tonight?" Or, "Bob said he can't pick me up tomorrow. Can you?"

When we respond to people with an active-constructive style, it dramatically improves the relationship. As we have seen, when relationships improve, our joy level goes up. Truthfully, why would we want to use any other style?

Of course, Paul did not wait for the other person to share good news before he celebrated them. He unearthed the good work of others from his own observations and went for it with active and constructive words. He not only praised the person directly, which is important, but he laid it out for others to see. In a way, I see it as a positive form of gossip.

As humans, we have an insatiable desire to share news with others: "Did you hear . . . ?" "Did you know . . . ?" Typically, the news we share is bad news. It is virtually impossible to stop doing this (James 3:6). But what if we got our fix by sharing the good news of another person's success behind their backs instead?

"Hey, did you know what Jack did the other day? He started mentoring a young boy at the local elementary school once a week in reading and recently got an award from the principal for the positive effect he is having on that kid's life! I'm not sure how he fits it all in with his work and all, but he seems to balance everything well. It sure does inspire me to want to do something like this."

And then, what if word got back to Jack that you were spreading this kind of news about him? It's true and it's positive. I don't know about you, but this would pick up my spirits and certainly deepen my relationship with the person who was bragging on me. You may not have a lot of friends like this, but we can all certainly strive to *be* that kind of friend to others. And when we do, it will cheer us up as well.

## LIFTING OTHERS UP

Bob Buford was an extremely successful businessman from East Texas. He owned a company that provided cable services to millions of homes (this was back in the days before YouTube, Hulu, and the like). The residual income amassed an amazing fortune for Bob.

Bob was also a devoted follower of Jesus and always had a sense that he should go into full-time Christian ministry, maybe as a pastor or a missionary. His mentor was Peter Drucker, the father of modern-day management and a devout follower of Jesus. Drucker convinced Bob that all Christians were in fact in full-time service to Christ in whatever station in life or field of work they were in, if they approached it for Christ's glory. Drucker went on to persuade Bob that he could make the greatest impact—"100X impact"—for the kingdom of God by staying in business and using it to fuel the success of pastors.

Bob made the decision to follow this advice a few years before I entered into my calling as a full-time pastor at the age of twenty-eight. He started an organization called Leadership Network "to convene leadership conversations and foster innovative movements that seek to activate the Church to 100X impact thereby transforming the world."[4]

My first church fell a few hundred people under the requirement to be invited into the community and conversation. I begged the executive director to let me participate, and they made an exception. The first event I attended was held on the beautiful grounds of the Navigators headquarters, tucked a stone's throw from the magnificent

Garden of the Gods in Colorado Springs, Colorado. The entire event was underwritten by Bob. The room was filled with the most innovative pastors in the country. Within minutes of the first gathering, I felt like I'd had three cans of Red Bull—my mind was spinning with ideas to change the world.

Bob once said, "The fruit of our work grows up on other people's trees."[5] This is precisely what Paul did as well: he found joy in other people's success.

As I look back on my thirty-five years of ministry, I can follow every successful venture I ever led back to Bob Buford. He mentored me, opened doors for me, encouraged me, and funded many of my projects. One instance in particular stands out in my memory.

Years ago, Bob convened three teams to work on measuring spiritual growth. I led one of the teams. Bob funded our gatherings and led us to the world's best resources. He passed on a book written by George Gallup Jr., of the famous Gallup Organization, entitled *The Saints Among Us*. I felt the book held the key to cracking the code on measuring spiritual growth. So, what did Bob do? He flew me to Princeton, New Jersey, to spend a few days brainstorming with . . . wait for it . . . George Gallup Jr.

George became a close friend, and a year later I published a tool to measure spiritual growth called *The Christian Life Profile Assessment*.[6] That tool has not only helped thousands of people move forward in their spiritual journey, but it has led me to be involved in a host of other projects and ministries that are too numerous to mention here.

A number of years ago, I had a meeting with Bob in his office in Dallas, Texas. I had prepared a gift to give him. It was a Waterford crystal apple placed on top of a wooden base with this inscription: "A piece of fruit from my tree that you grew." Bob could buy an island in the Caribbean and a private jet to visit it anytime he wanted, but the look on his face when I presented the apple to him was full of more joy than

I can express. Over the years that followed, I would visit Bob's office and find the crystal apple proudly displayed on his shelf for all to see.

Bob passed away in 2018. I attended the service in Dallas filled with the who's who in American Christianity. They were all there because of what Bob had done for them. You may have never heard of Bob Buford, but you likely know many of these people and have been positively impacted by the fruit of their work—work that Bob planted, watered, and nurtured.

I sat in the service and bawled uncontrollably as I recalled the memories and grieved my loss. I had lost someone who rooted for me for thirty years without fail. We often don't have many people like that in our lives. My heart was filled with overwhelming gratitude that brought me great joy.

Dr. Larry Crabb wrote, "A vision we give to others of who and what they could become has power when it echoes what the Spirit has already spoken into their souls."[7] How terribly satisfying to run point on offering that kind of a lift to others. Bob found joy in other people's success. Bob and the apostle Paul called us to do the same.

## THE JOY CHALLENGE

Paul invited us to actively and constructively share the good news of other people broadly. That is your Joy Challenge for today.

Be on the lookout today for good news that has recently happened to the people God has put in your life. Maybe someone got a promotion or finished a marathon or published an article or reached some goal they set or celebrated a significant anniversary. It could be something they did that helped someone else. Maybe that someone is you.

Once you have identified the good news, actively and constructively celebrate this success with that person. It can be as simple as sharing a few affirming statements. If you can meet with them personally, that would be best. Second best would be to FaceTime or Zoom with them. If you can't do either of those, you can call them, email them, or text them.

If it is appropriate, once you have spoken with the person, go a step further and broadcast this good news about them. You might share it at the dinner table or at a meeting at the office. Another option is to post it on your Facebook page or other social media platforms you use.

At the end of the day, record your thoughts about this experience in your journal. If you heard back from that person, reflect on how it made them feel. How about you? How did it make you feel?

> CARRY YOUR JOY CUBE WITH YOU ALL DAY
> AND CONTINUE MEMORIZING PHILIPPIANS
> 2:1–2, AS WELL AS REHEARSING YOUR FIRST
> MEMORY VERSE (PHILIPPIANS 1:21).

# DO RIGHT BY OTHER PEOPLE

*But I think it is necessary to send back to you Epaphroditus, my brother, co-worker and fellow soldier, who is also your messenger, whom you sent to take care of my needs. For he longs for all of you and is distressed because you heard he was ill. Indeed he was ill, and almost died. But God had mercy on him, and not on him only but also on me, to spare me sorrow upon sorrow. Therefore I am all the more eager to send him, so that when you see him again you may be glad and I may have less anxiety. So then, welcome him in the Lord with great joy, and honor people like him, because he almost died for the work of Christ. He risked his life to make up for the help you yourselves could not give me.*

**–PHILIPPIANS 2:25-30**

On the surface, this final paragraph in chapter 2 appears to be all about Paul sending Epaphroditus, the Philippian believer who delivered the financial gift to Paul, back to Philippi with this letter. But a deeper look shows us this passage is about the joy that comes from doing right by other people.

Take a closer look for yourself. Circle the following: "spare me sorrow upon sorrow," "glad," "less anxiety," and "great joy." What was transpiring here promised to lower the stress and increase the joy of Epaphroditus, the Philippian believers, and Paul himself.

In verse 25, Paul stated that he felt it was necessary to send him back. Apparently, Epaphroditus's mission was not only to deliver the material gift to Paul but to be on permanent loan to Paul as an assistant. Paul used five nouns to esteem this man:

- **BROTHER:** a fellow member of God's family
- **FELLOW WORKER:** an associate who works with Paul to get Christ's name into places it has not been mentioned
- **FELLOW SOLDIER:** a warrior fighting side by side with Paul to face conflicts together
- **YOUR ENVOY:** an equal apostle serving alongside Paul to get the message out (the word *envoy* is the Greek word *apostolos*, or "apostle")
- **MINISTER:** a priest performing sacred duties in his support of Paul

Paul told us in verse 26 that he was sending Epaphroditus back for two reasons. First, Epaphroditus "longs" for the Philippians. In a word, he was homesick. In case you were wondering, homesickness is a thing. It is estimated that 50 to 75 percent of the population has been affected by homesickness at some point in their life.[1] For me, it was my first semester away at college. Doctors tell us that homesickness is often manifested by symptoms of frequent crying, sleeping problems, difficulty concentrating, and withdrawal from people. Homesickness can turn into a full-blown case of clinical depression and even make one physically sick, with a lack of appetite, stomach problems, trouble sleeping, headaches, and fatigue. I think this happened to Epaphroditus.

The second reason Paul was sending him home gives us insight. Epaphroditus was "distressed" because the Philippians found out he was ill. The word Paul used here in the Greek is the same word used of Jesus in the garden of Gethsemane. We are told that Jesus was "distressed and troubled" (Mark 14:33). He said to his disciples, "My soul is overwhelmed with sorrow to the point of death" (Mark 14:34). The distress was so intense Jesus said it was taking him to the very brink of death. I think this may be what was happening to Epaphroditus. His homesickness slipped into chronic anxiety and depression, and it made him physically sick—"to the point of death."

Why would his distress and anxiety come from his knowing that the Philippians were aware of his illness? Well, one, I think he knew the Philippians loved him and were worried about him. He didn't want them to worry. But I think it was deeper than that. People who suffer from mental illness and breakdowns often feel embarrassed about their condition. Epaphroditus was sent to represent the church and to serve Paul for the long haul. The word of his mental and emotional struggle likely made him feel he had failed them, and this took his depression to a new level of despair.

In the next verse, Paul indicated that God showed mercy on Epaphroditus and healed him. This not only gave him relief but brought Paul relief as well. He said it spared him "sorrow upon sorrow" (v. 27). If you have ever been in a situation where someone you loved was struggling from depression and anxiety, then you know how painful it can be to watch them suffer. This phrase can also be translated "wave upon wave." If you have ever been out in the ocean or in a large lake when the water is rough, you may have felt this sensation of one wave hitting you after another. It is constant. It doesn't take a break. It causes your heart to race and can throw you into a bit of a panic.

Paul decided to do the right thing by Epaphroditus. He decided to give up the support for himself and send him back to Philippi. This would bring gladness to Epaphroditus's hurting heart, as well as to the Philippian believers. Paul also said it would relieve his own anxiety. Doing the right thing for other people has a way of doing that. Losing something for the sake of others has the profound effect of giving us back more, usually in the currency of increased inner joy and contentment.

Paul wrapped up this paragraph by instructing the Philippians to "welcome Epaphroditus with great joy" (v. 29). Remember, Epaphroditus was returning home, likely feeling he'd let them down. It would be a huge encouragement and an easing into his reentry to see a big, colorful "Welcome Home" sign stretched across the main entrance to Philippi. But it was more than balloons, a bounce house, and kosher hot dogs. When Epaphroditus came home with his head hung low, saying, "But I failed you guys. I feel so embarrassed," they needed to grab his cheeks and look him square in the eyes, prepared to tell him otherwise.

Paul said it well in his last sentence: "He risked his life to make up for the help you yourselves could not give me" (v. 30). For Paul, it wasn't just *what* Epaphroditus did; it was *why* he did it. Dr. Hawthorne wrote, "His was a self-renouncing motivation. He chose against himself for someone else."[2] In this way, Paul was comparing him to Christ from earlier in the chapter: "He made himself nothing. . . . [He] humbled himself by becoming obedient to death— even death on a cross!" (2:7–8). Epaphroditus risked his life to do something for Paul that the other Philippians weren't able to do. Maybe most weren't even willing to do. Hawthorne added, "The vigor of Paul's vocabulary here could not but totally overcome any remaining prejudice the Philippians may have had against Epaphroditus."

Paul chose a unique word for "risk" in the Greek for this very occasion, and I think it is quite clever. It is a gambling term that means "to throw down a stake." Epaphroditus played with very high stakes in order to come to the aid of Paul. But here is the clever part. The name Epaphroditus comes from the Greek goddess Aphrodite, who was the god of gamblers. Whenever a Greek made a bet, he cried out "epaphroditus," which means "favorite of Aphrodite," hoping to be blessed with gambler's luck in the throw of the dice.[3]

I can imagine Paul with a grin on his face as he wrote this letter, knowing that the Philippians would get his play on words when they read it. Epaphroditus gambled with his own life not only to deliver a financial gift over an eight-hundred-mile stretch of land and sea but to give up the comforts of his home to serve Paul on behalf of the Philippian believers. That kind of sacrifice will endear you to such a person. He got hit with an unexpected blast of homesickness that led to deep depression, which then led to a serious physical illness, but it doesn't change the courageous motive that caused him to roll the dice in the first place.

Out of a deep love for Epaphroditus, Paul did the right thing by him and sent him back home. Such an act increased everyone's joy!

## A WIN-WIN PROPOSITION

Recent brain research shows that God hardwired us for love and compassion. The more we give it out, the better things are for the people we help and the better it is for us. When we give to others, it activates the areas of the brain associated with pleasure, social connection, and trust. Altruistic behavior releases endorphins in the brain and boosts happiness for all of us.[4] It is a win-win proposition.

Charles Dickens's classic *A Christmas Carol* beautifully illustrates this truth. Ebenezer Scrooge is a stingy, closed-minded, untrusting, angry man with a great deal of hoarded wealth. He has an employee, Bob Cratchit, who is underpaid, underappreciated, and struggles to provide for the needs of his family, particularly his son Tiny Tim, who is struggling with a disease.

You know the story. Ebenezer gets visited by the Ghost of Christmas Past, then the Ghost of Christmas Present, and finally the Ghost of Christmas Future. Reliving the pain of his past and seeing the horror of his predicted future and the death of Tiny Tim creates an internal revival in his soul. Waking up from this horrible encounter on Christmas morning, Ebenezer Scrooge takes a new lease on life; he makes a 180-degree turn. He becomes a generous man. He decides to do the right thing by his employee, Bob Cratchit, by giving him a big raise and declaring that Tiny Tim will not die— and, in the end, he lives. If you haven't read the book or seen the movie, do so soon.

Note the transformation in Ebenezer's demeanor. He goes from being a slouched over, grouchy old man to one standing tall, smiling, engaging people, and full of joy. He definitely has activated his brain and released an avalanche of endorphins that filled him with joy. Why? When we do the right thing by other people, it not only increases their joy, but it also increases our joy at the same time in even greater measure. Jesus was right: "You're far happier giving than getting" (Acts 20:35 MSG).

Live a life of doing right by other people, and you will not die alone. Instead, like Ebenezer Scrooge learned, the celebration of your life will be quite a commemoration party!

# THE SLOUGH OF DESPOND, SACRIFICE, AND GREAT JOY

Several years ago, I suffered an awful confrontation with betrayal. A few "friends" broke a promise we had made to one another and threw me under the bus.[5] Like homesickness, all betrayal hurts, but not all betrayals lead to clinical depression. However, my betrayal led me into a deep well of depression. It seemed like each day I fell an inch deeper into the abyss.

As with Epaphroditus, this mental and emotional illness took its toll on my physical health. I couldn't sleep. I lost my appetite and quickly shed twenty pounds I didn't need to lose. I didn't feel like I was going to die, but I couldn't imagine a way out. This felt like my final stop.

My wife, now of over forty years, was my Paul. Rozanne did right by me. She remembered our marriage covenant: "For better or for worse, in sickness and in health." Over the next year as I shut down, she stepped up. The betrayal affected her life in a major way, too, but she brushed that to the side and focused on what was best for me. She never took the opportunity to grieve her loss, for fear it would send me even deeper into the Slough of Despond, like Christian in John Bunyan's famous allegory, *Pilgrim's Progress*.[6] I could, however, see it in her eyes. She was experiencing sorrow upon sorrow, wave upon wave, as she watched her once confident husband crumble before her eyes. I was so embarrassed, but I couldn't pull myself out of the tailspin. Like Epaphroditus, knowing she knew I was emotionally sick only made me sicker.

Finally, after eight months, an opportunity emerged that caused me to perk up just a little. Rozanne leaned in with her full support. Taking this opportunity would require a move from our home, away from our grandkids, away from the support of family and close friends, and away from warm weather. It wasn't lost on me that these are three things that bring her great joy in life. When I tried to turn the opportunity down, she kept pressing into it. So, after a great deal of deliberation and prayer, we made the decision to move.

Why? She was doing right by me at her expense. Just like Paul gave up his support and sent Epaphroditus back home, Rozanne gave up her support and moved away from home. Thanks to Rozanne, today I am fully healed and back up on the horse again, leading a very productive life.

I asked Rozanne the other day if it really was that painful to watch me struggle and wither away. She confirmed it was one of the hardest things she has ever witnessed. Like Paul, it filled her with anxiety. I then asked her if it brings her joy to know that her sacrifice was the key to my recovery. She smiled and simply said, "Yes!"

## THE JOY CHALLENGE

Your Joy Challenge today is to do right by someone else. An idea for what to do might come to you immediately. Great! But if you are struggling, here are three steps you can take:

1. Make a list of the people God has put into your life who need a break or a hand up. It could be a family member, a neighbor, a fellow student, a coworker, or maybe someone you barely know.

2. Identify what you can do to help. This often involves taking inventory of things you are responsible for, have access to, or own. (Perhaps you have authority to make things happen at work, or you know people who can help make things happen, or you own an extra car or a lake house you can offer, or you have physical strength to lend, or you own tools they can borrow.)

3. Pray for guidance, and then put the two things together. Identify a plan of execution, and then get after it before the sun goes down.

There is an endless sea of ideas for how you can do right by someone. One of the things I recently implemented as part of my doing right by Rozanne is being conscious to always open the car door for her. You just read all she did for me when I was struggling. This is just the tip of the iceberg. On top of that, she is my wife, and she has borne us four children and has given the best years of her life to raise them.

In the early years of courting, I used to open the door for her. But as time went by and the pace of life picked up, I stopped doing it. Getting four kids strapped into their seat belts and car seats was a major event every time. For the sake of efficiency, I justified the cessation of an important gesture of honor my wife deserved. One day, God brought this to my mind while I was praying. I needed to do right by her. So, that day, I got started and have been doing it ever since.

You can do the same for someone else. It can be a smaller thing like opening the car door or something bigger God brings to mind. Go ahead! Have fun!

CARRY YOUR JOY CUBE WITH YOU ALL DAY AND REHEARSE YOUR MEMORY VERSES: PHILIPPIANS 1:21 AND 2:1–2.

# PART 3

# JOY DESPITE YOUR PAST

## MEMORY VERSE

*Brothers and sisters, I do not consider myself yet to have taken hold of it. But one thing I do: Forgetting what is behind and straining toward what is ahead.*

**–PHILIPPIANS 3:13**

Raise your hand if you have a past. We all have one, don't we? For most people, our pasts are filled with a mixture of good things and bad things. Some of the good has come from what we have done—good choices we made, right actions we took. Some of the good has simply come to us—we had nothing to do with it. We were born into the right family. Breaks came our way. The wind blew in the right direction. The same can be said of the negative experiences in our past. Some have come from poor choices—destructive actions we have taken. Some of the bad has simply happened to us—we had nothing to do with it and yet it became part of our story. Wherever the good and the bad have come from, both can rob us of joy in our present life. This will be our focus in part 3 of the Joy Challenge.

This reminds me of an interesting study Dr. Martin Seligman conducted using dogs.[1] He placed some dogs, one at a time, in a closed box with no way to escape. He then placed another group of dogs, one at a time, in an open box with a clear path to escape. Dr. Seligman then applied an electrical shock to the floor of both boxes. The dogs in the open box learned quite quickly to jump out. The dogs in the closed box, realizing they had no chance of escape, soon gave up trying to get away from the shocks and laid down, accepting their situation. (Just as an aside, I don't have the constitution to do things like this.) Then, Dr. Seligman gathered both sets of dogs and placed them in a two-compartment box. One side issued an electrical shock, and the other side did not. All the dogs in the open box from the previous experience quickly learned to move to the next box. Interestingly, almost all the dogs who were in the closed box originally stayed in the box with the electrical current without ever trying to move into the box that would free them from their pain.

Psychologists call this *learned helplessness*. Our past conditions us to believe this is just the way things are. We think we are powerless over our past, so we just lie down and take it.

Have you ever wondered how the managers of a traveling circus keep the elephants from running away? When the elephant is a baby, the trainers tie its leash to a peg that is driven into the ground. The young elephant is unable to pull the peg from the earth and eventually stops trying. When the elephant grows into a massive creature, weighing as much as fourteen thousand pounds and standing as high as thirteen feet, they are capable of pulling the stake out of the ground and taking off. But they don't. Their past restrictions have defined the limits of their future—learned helplessness.

It works in a psychological way for humans. Maybe in our past, we were told that we were no good and wouldn't amount to much, and today that keeps us from believing in ourselves and having the confidence we need to move upward. Or perhaps we were betrayed by a friend or dumped by a girlfriend or boyfriend, and today it keeps us from trusting others and developing intimate friendships and healthy community. Or we may have experienced a traumatic event, like a tumble that caused serious injury, and today it keeps us from taking risks. Or we failed at something, like making the team, and today it keeps us from trying new adventures for fear we will fail again. Our past can not only dramatically limit our present and future progress, but it can rob us of joy, holding our happiness hostage.

For years, clinical psychology taught that the solution was to get into therapy and dredge up all your traumatic memories and drain your brain of them. In other words, people could free themselves from their past trauma if they could remove it through psychoanalysis. It turns out this was faulty thinking and didn't work for most people. We cannot erase the contents of our subconscious by merely calling it to mind.

The apostle Paul recommended an alternative path. Instead of trying to drain our brains of painful memories, we need to learn to rise above them. There is a way to have joy despite—and even because of—your past. We take our old, painful, dark memories and we create new, positive, meaningful new ones. The Bible would certainly agree.

Paul had a past just like you and me. Part of his past was filled with privilege and success; part of his past was filled with great pain and sorrow. He needed to find a way to live with both. He needed to find a way to not let the reptilian part of his brain[2] rule his life.

In chapter 3 of the book of Philippians, Paul presented us with five principles to increase our joy in spite of our past. Each one holds the promise of inching us forward to experience the complete joy of

Christ in us (John 15:11). It is a brand of joy that is different from what the world offers, a kind of joy that comes to terms with the pain of our past and realizes that its presence is a part of our story that can make us stronger and more effective to minister to a broken humanity—a transcendent joy.

Here is what I want you to do to prepare yourself for the next leg in the Joy Challenge: I want you to reflect on your past. Start by making a list of the good memories you have. Remember to include things that came about due to decisions and actions you took, as well as the good things that have come about in your life that were out of your control. Take some time to ponder how these events have helped you in your present life and how they may have hurt you and challenged your ability to experience joy.

It may be hard to grasp at first how good things in your past can rob you of joy today. Let me give you a few examples that may be true for those of you who had a positive family upbringing.

- **YOU WERE RAISED IN A FAMILY THAT SET GOOD BOUND-ARIES FOR YOU.** These guardrails kept you from being in places and doing things that get people into deep trouble, resulting in painful memories. Yet, if the boundaries kept you too sheltered from the world, there is a good chance you were not ready for the rudeness and temptations of the world when you ventured out on your own. This may have caused you to make some rookie mistakes that have been harmful to you and others and drained a little out of your joy account.

- **YOU WERE TOLD BY YOUR FAMILY AND TEACHERS THAT YOU CAN BE ANYTHING YOU WANT WHEN YOU GROW UP.** You grew up with a strong sense of self-esteem and confidence. That is a good thing. However, when it came time to decide what you wanted to be and do, you were paralyzed with too many options, and it has caused you to flounder in your life. That will rob you of joy. You now realize you weren't equipped by God to do anything you put your mind to. Welcome to humanity.

- **YOU COME FROM A WEALTHY FAMILY.** It looks like you will be the beneficiary of a nice trust fund. How can this not be a good thing? To be freed from financial worry is a blessing few people experience. However, you let it rob you of finding your sense of purpose and meaning on earth. It has stolen your drive and determination. This has the potential to rob you of joy.

- **YOU GREW UP WITH A MOM OR DAD OR BOTH WHO WERE NOT ONLY SUCCESSFUL BUT WERE SOMEWHAT FAMOUS.** This opened doors of opportunity for you that gave you an unfair advantage over others. Yet, you have found it hard to live in the shadow of your parents' popularity and the pressure to live up to high expectations for you to do the same.

Many of the good memories you have stored in your past don't have many downsides. My parents, for example, decided to move our family from southwest Pennsylvania to Cleveland, Ohio, when I was three years old. I had no say in the matter. Yet, that single decision, I believe, was a positive turning point in my life with zero downside. My decision to marry Rozanne over forty years ago when I was only twenty years old—brilliant move on my part—has also had nothing but upsides. That's okay. You'll probably have a mix of good memories that have upsides and downsides, as well as good memories that only have upsides.

Try to identify at least five good memories from your past.

Now, spend some time reflecting on the difficult memories from your past. I don't think you need as much help dredging these up. They usually raise their ugly heads without much effort. These can include events or circumstances that happened without your involvement or consent. These will also include decisions or actions you took of your own volition that you now regret and wish you could redo. Identify at least five of these experiences from your past.

Your past experiences, good and bad, may have had you chained to a peg that kept you from moving. Paul was saying to us, "Time to pull that peg out of the ground and get free." Maybe your past experiences and memories have you lying down in a box like the dogs we referred to earlier. Like them, you have given up hope that anything will change for you. You just lie down and take it—learned helplessness. But it doesn't have to be this way.

Paul was literally in such a box—a prison. Yet, he didn't lie down and take it. He transcended it and found joy despite his past. He wanted to show us how we can experience the same thing. Time to leave our broken past in the rearview mirror. Let's call it *learned hopefulness.*

> BE SURE TO CARRY YOUR JOY CUBE WITH YOU ALL DAY AND START MEMORIZING YOUR THIRD MEMORY VERSE: PHILIPPIANS 3:13.

# PRINCIPLE #11

# STAY CLEAR
# OF LEGALISM

*Further, my brothers and sisters, rejoice in the Lord! It is no trouble for me to write the same things to you again, and it is a safeguard for you. Watch out for those dogs, those evildoers, those mutilators of the flesh. For it is we who are the circumcision, we who serve God by his Spirit, who boast in Christ Jesus, and who put no confidence in the flesh—though I myself have reasons for such confidence.*

*If someone else thinks they have reasons to put confidence in the flesh, I have more: circumcised on the eighth day, of the people of Israel, of the tribe of Benjamin, a Hebrew of Hebrews; in regard to the law, a Pharisee; as for zeal, persecuting the church; as for righteousness based on the law, faultless.*

**—PHILIPPIANS 3:1-6**

Paul opened chapter 3 with the word *Further*. He gave us the impression he was going to move forward with some new information or his next point. Here it is: "Rejoice in the Lord!" (v. 1).

Paul knew his readers in Philippi would say, "Hey, wait a minute. You already made this point, like, multiple times. We thought you were going to tell us something new." Anticipating this, Paul wrote, "It is no trouble for me to write the same things to you again, and it is a safeguard for you" (v. 1). Paul was saying, "I have no problem repeating myself. Joy is my favorite topic, and it keeps me pumped up and positive while I hang out another day in this prison."

The various Greek words for *joy* appear 326 times in the New Testament, and Paul wrote 131 of them.[1] No doubt, he is the "Theologian of Joy." He thought about it all the time; he bathed in it.

Paul also said that he kept bringing up joy because "it is a safeguard for you" (v.1). What does that mean? It is very dangerous to go through a day without proactively practicing the principles of joy he presented in this letter. Each day our circumstances, other people, our past, and our propensity to worry seek to steal our joy. We need a counterattack strategy. One of the best approaches is to wake up each day rejoicing in the Lord! That is what the twenty principles of the Joy Challenge are all about. So, let's keep pressing onward.

Then, out of nowhere, it seems, Paul made a serious shift in topic and mood. In verse 2, it would appear he abandoned the topic of joy altogether, but that is not what he was doing. He was addressing one of the biggest joy robbers of all: legalism. This brings us to our next joy principle: Stay Clear of Legalism.

What does legalism have to do with finding joy despite our past? Many new Christians in the first century came out of the Jewish religion steeped in the laws of the Old Testament. This is how they were raised. As they moved forward in their new faith, which was rooted in grace, the tendency toward legalism would raise its ugly head and make them feel guilty. Even if they were able to move forward, family members and clerics would have been putting pressure on them to go backward. Throughout my thirty-plus years of ministry I have seen many, many Christians struggle to leave behind their pasts, the legalistic roots they were raised in. Roots that tell them they need to adhere to the rules that someone made up to be good enough for God to love them. It existed in the days of Paul in the first century, and it still exists today in the twenty-first century.

With no holds barred, Paul barked, "Watch out for those dogs, those mutilators of the flesh" (v. 2). Yikes! It may not sound like it to you in English, but this is pretty rough language in the Greek. The truth is, the translators were unwilling to give us the full force of the language Paul used about these people. If I translated from the Greek into the lay language of today, you might get offended and stop reading right here. Many moms might opt to put him in a time out. But Paul was upset, and for good reason. He was fighting for our joy!

The *Oxford English Dictionary* defines legalism as an "excessive adherence to law or formula."[2] Laws and formulas are good and have their place. It is when they get excessive that we have a problem. From a theological sense, legalism is a dependence on the moral laws of God over a personal relationship with God and compassion for other people. Jesus confronted this all the time in the Gospels with the religious leaders, particularly around the subject of the Sabbath. They got extremely mad at Jesus when he showed compassion to a hurting person and healed them on the Sabbath. On one occasion, Jesus responded,

> You hypocrites, does not each of you on the Sabbath untie his ox or his donkey from the stall and lead him away to water him? And this woman, a daughter of Abraham as she is, whom Satan has bound for eighteen long years, should she not have been released from this bond on the Sabbath day? (Luke 13:15–16 NASB)

There are 613 laws in the Old Testament that are from God and are good and serve an important purpose. Some of the laws are moral and deal primarily with a person's conduct, such as the famous Ten Commandments. They teach us how we are to go about loving God and loving our neighbor. They also expose our need for Christ. They illuminate our inability to keep them. They give our sinful actions, reactions, and behavior a name. Other laws are ceremonial, meaning they exist to point people to the coming of Christ, like animal sacrifices, special feasts and festivals, dietary and clothing restrictions, and the observance of special days (like the Sabbath).

The Bible clearly tells us that Jesus didn't abolish the law but fulfilled it (Matthew 5:17). While we still seek to live by the moral code of God in the Old Testament (like "do not murder" and "honor your father and mother"), keeping the law no longer determines our eternal fate. Jesus fulfilled the requirement of the law for us. He perfectly kept the moral law of God and is the full manifestation of all the ceremonial laws intended to teach us. Faith in Jesus frees us from the burden of the law and secures our destiny. We are not obligated to observe the ceremonial laws because they fulfilled their purpose by pointing us to Christ. For example, we don't offer animal sacrifices anymore because Christ came and offered the once-and-for-all sacrifice for sin (Hebrew 10:8–14). We are also no longer required to keep the Sabbath (Friday sundown to Saturday sundown), although the practice of rest from work one day a week has proven to be good for us (Mark 2:27).

When Paul was writing this letter, a group of Jewish legalists were infiltrating the church at Philippi, teaching that people had to keep the law to have a right relationship with God. Particularly, they were wanting the Greek men and boys to be circumcised, which is why Paul called them "mutilators of the flesh" (v. 2). These religious canines were weighing the believers down with a performance-based religion, and it made Paul very angry.

Paul may have been known as the Theologian of Joy, but he was also known as the Theologian of Grace. Of the 153 times the word *grace* appears in the New Testament, 83 of them came from Paul. It is significant that the word for "joy" (*chara*) and the word for "grace" (*charis*) are derived from the same root. The two concepts are linked. One produces the other.

Legalism, on the other hand, produces guilt and competition. Legalism keeps a scorecard, and the trophy goes to the best performer, the best religious athlete. In the end, legalists don't boast of what Christ has done for them but boast in their flesh, or their accomplishments over others.

Paul felt so deeply about this because this was the game he once played in his past. In fact, he was pretty good at it. You might say he was an expert in it. In verses 4–6, Paul showed us his birth certificate. He was born into the right family; he was a blue blood, a hoity toity somebody who had the background and advantage anyone would envy. Not only that, but he made the most of what he had. He ran circles around everybody on keeping the Sabbath, eating the right foods, and practicing ceremonial cleanings. He graduated magna cum laude from Jerusalem High and was on the cover of both *Jewish People Magazine* and *Religious Sports Illustrated* on numerous occasions. He also persecuted the church that was such a threat to religious authorities. He actively led the way in tracking down Christians (people driven by grace) to imprison them and to kill them. At the end of his bragging spree in this passage, he gave himself a score: "as for righteousness based on the law, faultless" (v. 6).

All this left Paul exhausted and covered in guilt. Legalism always does that. But, once he discovered grace, he left legalism in his rearview mirror and invited us to do the same. He had zero tolerance for people trying to hang this weight around anyone's neck. It's a form of abuse, for sure. So, Paul got a little red in the cheeks as he wrote about it. The hairs on the back of his neck stood straight up. He clenched his teeth and pressed a little harder with his quill on the scroll and let these guys have it. Legalism doesn't work to establish a right relationship with God—only Jesus can do that. Legalism and joy cannot coexist. One of the two has to go bye-bye. Legalism will rob you and the people you hang around of your ability to rejoice in the Lord! This was not going to happen under Paul's watch.

And yet legalism is alive and well in the church today. We don't squabble about the same issues, like circumcision and a kosher diet, but the operating principles are the same. Here are the common traits of a modern legalist. A legalist

- loves rules more than people.
- loves being right more than being kind.
- looks down on people who are not like them.
- wants others to clean up before they come in.
- struggles with the fact that the thief on the cross got in under the wire (Luke 23:34–43).
- loves when the preacher scolds people for things they don't struggle with personally (or at least not in public).
- teaches human traditions as if they were the Word of God (Mark 7:8).

Most legalists don't know they are legalists. They believe they are honoring God and defending the purity of God's Word. They walk around with an air of righteousness. There is a fine line between justice and legalism. Legalists appear to want things to be fair and equal, but they drain out all the grace and compassion. Get a group of legalists together, and you'll have a hot mess on your hands. They sit around and fuel one another's passions and build one another up by tearing others down. You often find a tribe of legalists saying things like "Can you believe those people?" and "Thank God I am not like those people" (Luke 18:11).

Paul's advice: You want to increase your joy? Live in grace and don't be a legalist groupie.

## THE *TETRIS* EFFECT

There is a phenomenon psychologists have dubbed "the *Tetris* Effect." Named after the famous tile-matching video game created in 1984, this effect takes place when people spend so much time and attention with an activity that it begins to affect their thoughts, mental images, and dreams.[3] Gamers start to see the world through the lens of shapes and how they might fit together. They see images of tiles falling from the sky outside the game, including when they sleep. They dream in tiles. The same effect happens outside of video games and can produce what Shawn Achor calls "the Negative *Tetris* Effect."[4]

For example, tax auditors spend all day scanning tax forms for errors. Over time, like what happens with excessive hours playing *Tetris*, their brains become wired to look for mistakes. That is super helpful when it comes to job performance, but it is another thing when it spills into other areas of their life. They start looking for mistakes and errors everywhere, and it starts to undermine their relationships at work and home. Achor cites a few examples from a tax firm he consulted for:

> In performance reviews, they noticed only the faults of their team members, never their strengths. When they went home to their families, they noticed only the C's on their kid's report cards, never the A's. When they ate at restaurants, they could only notice that the potatoes were underdone—never that the steak was cooked perfectly.[5]

One auditor confessed that he made an Excel spreadsheet listing all the mistakes his wife had made over the previous six weeks. I would have paid big money to see her response when he presented it to her.

Achor noted that a similar phenomenon exists among lawyers who have been trained to look for flaws in arguments. It turns out lawyers are 3.6 times more likely to suffer from major depressive disorders than those with other occupations.[6] They suffer from a lack of joy. Achor talked to lawyers who confessed a habit of deposing their children when they got home from work and thinking of time with their spouse in billable hours. As they say in Texas, "That dog won't hunt."

What happens to gamers, tax auditors, and lawyers can most definitely happen to people of faith. We get raised in an environment of legalism, whether in the home or at church, and our brain is trained to look for errors and flaws in others. Little by little, without much notice, like the frog in a pot of boiling water, our brains get cooked on legalism. We take this into our relationships at home, in the neighborhood, at work, at church, and even when we are watching the evening news, and it destroys relationships, creates division and tension, and robs the joy of everyone within striking distance of our attitude.

## LIVING A DOUBLE LIFE

Interestingly, legalists are often busted for living a double life. They say one thing in public and do another in private.

For example, the leader of a vegetarian society just couldn't control himself anymore. He felt he needed to try some pork, just to see what it tasted like. So, one summer day, he told the members of the society that he was going on a vacation. He drove out of town to the nearest restaurant. Just a few minutes after settling in at his table, he heard someone call his name and, to his chagrin, he saw one of his fellow members walking toward him. At that same moment, the waiter walked over with a huge platter, holding a full roasted pig with an apple in its mouth. "Isn't that something?" said the leader after only a moment's pause. "All I do is order an apple and look at what it comes with!"

Busted.

Now, I personally find that funny, but the truth is, legalism is not at all funny when you live it day in and day out. Legalists are miserable people who walk around like they have been sucking on lemons.

Don't be that guy; don't be that gal. If your closest friends are legalists, time to find some new friends. Stay clear of legalism!

## THE JOY CHALLENGE

Our Joy Challenge today has two parts to it, with the goal of creating a positive *Tetris* Effect.

First, I want you to evaluate your life against the seven traits of a legalist using the following criteria. Put a "1" next to the trait you think is the hardest for you. Put a "2" next to the one that is the next hardest for you. Keep going until you get to the one that least represents you and mark it with the number 7.

Now, take some time to journal your thoughts about your ratings. Start by celebrating your number seven rating. Why is this not true of you? Thank God for this. Then go to the one you ranked as number one. Write out why this one is truer of you than the others. What is the underlying driver of this attitude? As you go through the day, be mindful of this in your activities and encounters with others. You may even want to share this with a trusted friend and ask them to pray for you and help you grow in this area.

The second part of your challenge for today is to take the same list of traits and think through the key relationships in your life: at home, in your neighborhood, at school, at church, in your friendship circles. Do you have any people or groups of people in your life that struggle with these traits? Do you have any people or groups of people in your life that don't struggle with the traits of a legalist? Write down your thoughts.

Once you have done this, find some time to share your thoughts with at least one person who is a grace-giver to you. Maybe show them the list and tell them how much joy they bring you. Then, if you have any person or group of people who really struggle with these qualities and you find bring you down, consider how you will apply Paul's advice and "stay clear of the legalist."

## 7 Traits of a Legalist

\_\_ Loves rules more than the person

\_\_ Loves being right more than being kind

\_\_ Looks down on people who are not like them

\_\_ Wants others to clean up before they come in

\_\_ Struggles with the fact that the thief on the cross got in under the wire

\_\_ Loves when the preacher scolds people for things they don't struggle with personally

\_\_ Teaches human traditions as if they were the Word of God

CARRY YOUR JOY CUBE WITH YOU EVERYWHERE YOU GO TODAY. MAKE SURE YOU POP IT OPEN SO YOU AND OTHERS CAN KEEP THE PRINCIPLES EVER BEFORE YOU. DON'T FORGET TO GO OVER YOUR MEMORY VERSE FOR THIS SECTION: PHILIPPIANS 3:13.

# PRINCIPLE #12

# RECALCULATE WHAT REALLY MATTERS

*But whatever were gains to me I now consider loss for the sake of Christ. What is more, I consider everything a loss because of the surpassing worth of knowing Christ Jesus my Lord, for whose sake I have lost all things. I consider them garbage, that I may gain Christ and be found in him, not having a righteousness of my own that comes from the law, but that which is through faith in Christ—the righteousness that comes from God on the basis of faith. I want to know Christ—yes, to know the power of his resurrection and participation in his sufferings, becoming like him in his death, and so, somehow, attaining to the resurrection from the dead.*

**–PHILIPPIANS 3:7-11**

In this powerful passage Paul put on his spiritual accounting hat. He talked about profits and losses and assets and liabilities and account balances and transfers, but they have nothing to do with one's financial standing and net worth and everything to do with our right standing before God and our self-worth. Paul's Joy Challenge for us today is all about recalculating what really matters.

In this paragraph, Paul gave us his who's who biography. He had the right pedigree and went to the right schools and got the right degrees. He graduated top of his class. He outwitted and outworked everyone and had the accolades to prove it. Paul was a big deal. For most of Paul's life, he saw these things as gains in his ledger of importance and prominence. But then he met Jesus on the road to Damascus and did some serious recalculating on what really mattered in his life.

The things he thought were gains bankrupted him spiritually. No doubt the words of Jesus must have been ringing in his mind: "What will it profit a man if he gains the whole world, and loses his own soul?" (Mark 8:36 NKJV). The name of Jesus appears three times in the first two verses of this passage. The person of Jesus and a personal relationship with Jesus were what Paul now considered to be of great value. This was such a radical shift. He had despised Jesus, and now Jesus meant everything to Paul. So, Paul up and walked away from it all cold turkey. He cut his losses and moved on to what really mattered. He put all his investments into a single account: the life of a follower of Jesus.

Notice that Paul used the word *consider* twice in verse 8. You can't see this in the English, but in the Greek he wrote the same word in two different tenses. The first time he used this verb, he was saying that on one particular day he settled things in his mind and made his final decision to shift his net worth from his performance to his position in Jesus. The second time he used the word he altered the tense of the verb. This time it meant he was continuously making this decision every day not to depend on himself, who he was, the things he possessed, or what he had accomplished.

He considered the things he valued in the past as "garbage." This is a pretty gross word in the Greek language. The transliteration of the word is *skubala*, and it refers to filth, a half-eaten corpse, excrement, or lumps of manure. I think this can be classified as onomatopoeia, a word that sounds like its meaning. Say it out loud a few times and see if you don't agree. Paul was once again not mincing words. He was not holding back on how he truly felt.

When Paul referred to the "surpassing worth of knowing Christ Jesus my Lord," he was careful in his selection of words. In the Greek he had several choices for the word *knowing*. He could have chosen a word that means "to comprehend mentally." He could have chosen a word to describe his relationship with Jesus that means "to know by acquaintance." He could have chosen a word that refers to facts: "Here are the analytics on Jesus." But he chose a word that means "to know experientially."[1] The knowledge of Christ no doubt involves one's thoughts and facts, but in its distinctive biblical usage, it may be said to involve primarily one's heart.[2] For Paul, this isn't a religion, which he had just left, but a relationship. This distinction really mattered to Paul, as it should to us.

In verse 9, Paul declared that he wanted to "be found in him, not having a righteousness of my own that comes from the law, but that which is through faith in Christ—the righteousness that comes from God on the basis of faith." He was referring to the time when we all will stand before God and be judged. He didn't want to be judged on the basis of his own merits but on the merits of Christ. Here we have another accounting metaphor. It's technically called "imputation" and refers to the charging of one's account. Here God imputes or puts Christ's record on my account and puts my record on Christ's account. When we stand before God, we are given Christ's record as though it were ours. Christ took our record and was issued the death penalty in our place. Now, that is a demonstration of grace that should increase our joy!

Paul wrapped up his thoughts in verses 10 and 11, reinforcing how much he wanted to know Christ experientially. Specifically, he wanted "to know the power of his resurrection and participation in his suffering, becoming like him in his death, and so, somehow, attaining to the resurrection from the dead." Paul wanted to experience Christ by entering into his suffering and death. This was symbolized spiritually when he was baptized. Going under the water represents our death and the end of our association with Adam, who got us into this mess. Coming out of the water represents our spiritual birth into our new relationship with Jesus, the Second Adam (Romans 6:2–11). When we believe in Jesus and are baptized, the same thing happens to us. In this way, we enter into his suffering and death.

But it doesn't stop there. Paul also wanted to know the power of Christ's resurrection and attain to the resurrection from the dead. In Ephesians 1:19–20, Paul told us that the same power that raised Jesus from the dead lives in us. When we align our lives with the will of God and yield our lives to the Spirit of God within us, it unleashes the power of God in and through us to do way more than we could do in our own strength. That should certainly fire up our desire to walk with God and pick up our spirits and increase our joy.

Attaining to the resurrection from the dead carries the idea a step further. When Jesus returns to establish his kingdom, all of those who have placed their faith in Christ will receive an imperishable, resurrected body like Jesus did three days after his crucifixion. When this happens to us who believe, we will reign with him on the new earth forever and ever. There is no possible way this truth can do anything but fire us up with hope and joy. No matter how difficult today seems, like sitting in prison for your faith, it pales in comparison to how our story ends—or rather, begins.

John, who was the first of the disciples to arrive at the empty tomb, wrote in his first letter, "We saw it, we heard it, and now we're telling you so you can experience it along with us, this experience of communion with the Father and his Son, Jesus Christ. Our motive for writing is simply this: We want you to enjoy this, too. Your joy will double our joy!" (1 John 1:3–4 MSG).

Paul's message to us today is simply this: If we want to increase our joy despite our past, we need to recalculate what really matters. We need to cut our losses in the things we once trusted in and make a shift to a personal relationship with Jesus Christ. As Jim Elliot, a martyred missionary to the Quechua people, said, "He is no fool who gives what he cannot keep, to gain that which he cannot lose."[3]

## IDENTITY AND WORTH

At the very foundation of this entire passage in Philippians is the subject of our identity (who we are) and our worth (why we matter). No one can possibly experience joy if they do not have a satisfying answer to both questions.

I think the popular concept of seeking self-worth by turning inward is a bit flawed. If I am struggling with my identity and a sense of my worth and I look within myself to find it, I don't think that works. It would be like going to yourself for one hundred dollars when you don't have one hundred dollars. In the same way, we can't go to ourselves to find worth if we don't feel worthy.

Identity and worth that lead to the experience of joy is a communal thing. Neuro-theologian Jim Wilder wrote, "In the human brain, identity and character are formed by who we love."[4] The orbital prefrontal cortex is located just behind our eye sockets. Whenever people make eye contact with us and we can see on their faces that they are pleased with us and want to be with us, it stimulates this part of the brain. That experience is the feeling of joy. But it can be disrupted when you don't receive this kind of acceptance early on.

You have likely heard about people who suffer from attachment disorder. When they were younger, starting at six months of age when one's sight and the orbital prefrontal cortex develops, they did not have people in their life who looked at them in this way. This left them with a low self-image, a struggle to trust, a resistance to affection, and anger issues. The same thing can happen when it comes to our relationship with God. We need to know we are loved and accepted and delighted in by him. When we don't have that, we are prone to developing identity issues.

This is what was so powerful when the Aaronic blessing was said over the people in the Old Testament and when it is sung over people today. God instructed Moses to have his brother, the priest, speak this blessing over the people of Israel:

> The LORD bless you and keep you;
> The LORD make his face shine upon you and be
>    gracious to you;
> The LORD turn his face toward you and give you peace.
>
> **(NUMBERS 6:24-26)**

As we hear these words spoken over us and take in the reality that God's face is looking at us and he loves us and is offering us grace and peace, it stimulates our brains and releases joy. I believe this is the same thing Paul was getting at in his letter to the people living in the ancient city of Corinth when he wrote, "For God, who said, 'Let light shine out of darkness,' made his light shine in our hearts to give us the light of the knowledge of God's glory displayed in the face of Christ" (2 Corinthians 4:6).

It is one thing for a parent, a mate, a sibling, or a good friend to look us in the face and let us know they are pleased with us and glad to be with us. What a blessing. It is another thing altogether to have Jesus, the Son of God, look at us and declare that we are so loved that he came to earth and wrapped himself in frail flesh and died for us so we could live with him for eternity through faith. Regardless of what the legalists say, he is pleased with us. He turns his face toward us and gives us peace. That daily declaration fires up my brain and releases a crazy amount of joy.

This is what Paul was talking about. When we are in desperate need of identity and worth, instead of turning to ourselves for what we don't have to give, we can turn to the one who has everything and freely gives us what we need. Paul cut his losses with his past strategy and put all his focus and energy on the face of Jesus to establish his identity and worth. He shifted his life from a performance-based model to a position-based model.

The performance-based model rests completely on ourselves to impress others in such a way that they applaud us. This is the strategy most of us work from, and it is utterly exhausting. If you happen to achieve a high degree of success, you now have the lifelong burden of sustaining it. I need a nap just thinking about it. The position-based model, on the other hand, is relational. It declares, "I am significant because of my position as a child of God. My identity and worth are not up for grabs today but are secure in my unconditional relationship with Jesus Christ. Therefore, I take a deep breath and release it, knowing that I am loved by God. I see the sparkle in Jesus' eye that he is happy to be with me."

John's wishes expressed in 1 John 1:3 have come true. My communion with God and his Son, Jesus Christ, has brought me joy.

# FEELING GOD'S PLEASURE

The Best Picture award at the 1981 Oscars went to the film *Chariots of Fire*. It is the true story of two runners, Eric Liddell and Harold Abrahams. The first time they met up, Eric beat Harold and it unnerved Harold to no end. They both ended up making the team to run for the British in the 1924 Summer Olympics.

As they were traveling by boat from Britain to Paris, Eric, a devout follower of Jesus, found out his event, the 100-meter race, was to be held on a Sunday. Out of conviction to honor the Lord's Day, he told the committee he was pulling out of the race. This infuriated them, but Eric held his ground. Fortunately, another runner, who had already won a medal, gave Eric his spot in the 400-meter race on Thursday.

Harold ended up running the 100-meter race on Sunday without Eric in the lineup and won the gold. On Thursday, Eric Liddell ran the 400-meter race and, though he was not expected to win the race because of its distance, he took the gold.

The first time I watched this movie I didn't get it. Two guys ran two different races and they both won. What's the point? The second time I watched it, I got it. It was not the outcome of the race that mattered but why they ran in the first place.

Harold Abrahams ran to prove who he was. In a scene before the race, he is lying on the massage table talking to his fellow racer, Aubrey Montague. He says to Aubrey, "And now in one hour's time, I will be out there again. I will raise my eyes and look down that corridor, four feet wide, with ten lonely seconds to justify my whole existence. But will I? Aubrey, I've known the fear of losing but now I am almost too frightened to win."[5] Why was he frightened? What if there wasn't anything on the other side that was worthwhile? After the race, he and his trainer, Sam Mussabini, go out and get drunk.

Eric Liddell, on the other hand, did not run to prove who he was but to express who he already knew he was. He told his sister earlier in the movie, "I believe God made me for a purpose . . . But he also made me fast, and when I run I feel his pleasure."[6] Eric felt the face of God turned toward him as he was running, and he felt God's blessing. This stimulated Eric's orbital prefrontal cortex and released all kinds of joy within him. If you haven't watched the movie, you should. You can visibly see when he feels the pleasure of God upon him.

Harold Abrahams ran with a performance-based mindset: "I will win and prove to myself and the world that I am a somebody." Eric Liddell ran from a position-based mindset: "I will run because, whether I win or lose, God is pleased with me and I express to the world that Jesus is a somebody."

Can you feel the immense difference between the two approaches to life? The apostle Paul finally did, and he ditched the performance-based strategy he'd operated from in his past that relied completely on him and shifted to a position-based strategy that relied on the record of Jesus. He then invited us to do the same.

## THE JOY CHALLENGE

The Aaronic blessings of Numbers 6:24–26 have been put to music by several artists. The first was written and performed by Christian artist Michael Card, entitled "Barocha." The second was written by Cody Carnes and Kari Jobe, entitled "The Blessing." For your challenge today, find these songs on whatever platform you use. Listen to both songs and pick the style that best fits you. Then, sometime today, whether in the morning or on your lunch break or in the evening, schedule a time and place with no distractions and listen to the song from start to finish. You can do this alone or invite others into the experience.

Before you start the song, take some deep breaths to release any tension you may have. Assume a posture that best puts you into a mood to receive. Whisper a prayer to God that you are ready to receive his blessing. Close your eyes and imagine Jesus looking into your eyes with an expression of pure love and delight to spend time with you. Start the music and take in the reality of your position as a child of God.

When you're done, take some time to write your thoughts in your journal. Thank God for seeing you, loving you, and affirming you. Thank God for blessing you. What did this experience do for your joy levels?

> CARRY YOUR JOY CUBE WITH YOU EVERYWHERE YOU GO TODAY. MAKE SURE YOU POP IT OPEN SO YOU AND OTHERS CAN KEEP THE PRINCIPLES EVER BEFORE YOU. DON'T FORGET TO GO OVER YOUR MEMORY VERSE FOR THIS SECTION: PHILIPPIANS 3:13.

# PRINCIPLE #13

# PUT THE PAST BEHIND YOU

*Not that I have already obtained all this, or have already arrived at my goal, but I press on to take hold of that for which Christ Jesus took hold of me. Brothers and sisters, I do not consider myself yet to have taken hold of it. But one thing I do: Forgetting what is behind.*

**–PHILIPPIANS 3:12-13**

**P**aul introduced us to the next joy principle by writing, "Not that I have already obtained all this." All what? In the last chapter, Paul increased his joy by reevaluating what really matters. He made the decision to cut his losses on his previous way of life, which was performance-based, and shift to a position-based model, which put all his eggs in the basket of knowing Jesus. A seismic shift from "what you do" to "who you know."

Paul's new modus operandi was daily plumbing the depths of this relationship. He was looking into the face of Jesus and seeing the sparkle in Jesus' eyes for him. This was sending his joy levels through the roof despite his circumstances, other people, and even his past. When he wrote, "Not that I have already obtained all this," Paul was saying, "I haven't gotten to the bottom of all this relationship offers." It is likely impossible in this life to do so. Dr. Hawthorne added, "To know the incomprehensible greatness of Christ demands a lifetime of arduous inquiry."[1] Paul hadn't gotten there yet, but he wanted to because each step closer increased his experience with this indescribable inner contentment and sense of purpose.

So, Paul "pressed on." This word in the Greek is the language of the hunter. It means "to pursue," "to hunt down," "to chase." This is what Jesus did with Paul. He hunted him down on the road to Damascus in pursuit of a personal relationship with him (Acts 9:1–19). Paul then wanted to pursue Jesus like Jesus pursued Paul. He was singing the song of the psalmist: "As the deer pants for streams of water, so my soul pants for you, my God" (Psalm 42:1). This was all about growing in his relationship with Christ. He was satisfied that he had a relationship with Jesus but not with his walk in Jesus. Warren Wiersbe wrote, "A sanctified dissatisfaction is the first essential to progress in the Christian race."[2] Paul wanted more of what was available in Christ, so he was going after it with gusto.

With his goal clearly and passionately set, he wrote, "But one thing I do . . ." (v. 13). I don't know about you, but I love that sense of extreme focus and determination. Instead of getting paralysis from analysis, he bypassed all the complexity and made his decision: "This will be my singular focus."

So, what is the "one thing" Paul was going to zero in on in order to get to know Christ better so he could increase his joy? Well, it has two parts to it. We will cover the second action step in our next chapter. The first actionable item in his decision tree is "forgetting what is behind . . ." This is an essential principle for the successful runner. When a runner looks behind them as they race, they decrease their pace by 28 percent.[3] And you know what happens when you reduce your pace by 28 percent—you lose the race. This same truth applies in everyday life, particularly our spiritual life. When we keep looking behind us, it slows our progress toward the main goal. We've got to stop doing that. So, our next principle to increase our joy is to put the past behind us.

When Paul said he was forgetting what was behind, he did not mean he was failing to remember. In reality, it is impossible to forget our past. Plus, it is helpful to remember our past, because it is a great teacher. What hurts us the most, often teaches us the most. We all have a past filled with pain, hurt, betrayal, broken promises, illnesses, death, trauma, and poor decisions. The key is not to waste the value of our past while also not getting stuck there. Someone once said, "He who doesn't learn from his past is doomed to repeat it."

I once had a favorite coffee mug. I drank every cup of coffee out of this mug. One day, a member of my staff accidently hit it and it fell to the ground, smashing into a million pieces (okay, maybe thirty pieces). I know you are not supposed to cry over spilled milk, but this was more than milk; this was my valued mug that contained the milk. That seemed different to me.

The next day, I went out of town. When I came back a week later, to my surprise, the mug was back on my desk. It was put back together with gold-colored glue and came with a note of apology and explanation. The Japanese art form called *kintsugi* puts broken pieces back together with gold, reminding us that we all have imperfections and flaws in our story but, if we have the right perspective, we can see how our brokenness can make us stronger, better, and even a more beautiful, empathetic person. We need to let the past be our teacher. Paul was definitely for this.

Paul had a lot in his past to leave behind. First, he had to get past his successes. Maybe you've heard the old adage "He climbed the ladder of success, only to find the ladder leaning against the wrong wall." There is nothing wrong with success, but if it leads you to the wrong place, you have to climb down the ladder and not look back. The same is true for us. We can become shackled by our successes.

For some of us, it led us up the wrong ladder. Our success is unidimensional rather than multidimensional.[4] We have a sense of purpose that comes from our work, but we acquired it at the cost of our health and our relationships—not good. Climb down, learn from it, and move on.

For others, we have let our past successes form a layer of pride and arrogance in us. For years now, we may not have picked up on it, but others have. And they really don't like being around us unless they have to (like to get a paycheck or because they are related to us). Climb down, learn from it, and move on.

For others, our past successes have caused us to think our best days are behind us. This is true for many older people. We find ourselves waking up without any compelling goals for the day. We have given up. We have put our life in neutral. Our past successes have crippled us, hurt us, or hurt others. We need to learn from them and then move on.

Paul also had to get past the things he had done wrong. His persecution, imprisonment, and even execution of Christians had to stand out above them all. Given how his relationship with Jesus meant absolutely everything to him now, you can imagine how hard this was to overcome so he could experience the forgiveness of God. It is one thing for God to forgive us; it is another thing for us to forgive ourselves.

We have all made poor decisions and done bad things that paralyze us with guilt. Bad things have also happened to us that overwhelm us with despair. The truth is, that tree has fallen where it has fallen, and we can't do anything about it. People who get stuck in the past are sad and miserable. People who learn from the past but keep moving forward are happy, vibrant folks filled with joy. That's what Paul wanted for himself. That is what Paul wanted for us.

## NEUROPLASTICITY AND THE RECIPE FOR JOY

If a neurologist were sitting with Paul in a panel discussion, he would follow up Paul's comments by saying, "I can tell you why this works to increase your joy."

Science has made a new discovery about our brains within the last two decades. Before this empirical revelation, scientists considered the brain to be fixed and unchangeable after a certain age (usually five years of age). This is now considered faulty thinking, and the theory has been replaced with the concept of neuroplasticity. *Plasticity* means "the capacity for being molded or altered."[5] In the simplest of terms, it means that we can change from the inside out. Can I get an amen?

In Paul's letter to the Roman Christians, he called this "the renewing of your mind" (Romans 12:2). The J. B. Phillips translation states it well:

> Don't let the world around you squeeze you into its own mould, but let God re-mould your minds from within, so that you may prove in practice that the plan of God for you is good, meets all his demands and moves towards the goal of true maturity.

The world can conform or squeeze us into their mold from the outside in, but we have the power to remold our minds from the inside out. The Greek word Paul used in Romans 12:2 is *metamorphous*. Like a caterpillar in the cocoon is transformed from the inside out, so our minds in concert with the Spirit of God within can be transformed from the inside out by the physical and spiritual practices we engage daily that lead to our desired outcome: true maturity.

Dr. Caroline Leaf's groundbreaking work in the study of neuroplasticity offers us much hope for happiness. It is true that the decisions and way of life of the people of our past, our family, have affected our lives today. Their decisions shaped their genes, and their genes were passed to us. Leaf wrote, "Science and Scripture both show how the results of our decisions pass through the sperm and ova to the next four generations, profoundly affecting their choices and lifestyles."[6] This lines up with the teaching of Scripture: "He punishes the children and their children for the sin of the parents to the third and fourth generation" (Exodus 34:7).

Our brains and bodies have mysteriously inherited the decisions and choices of our families of origin, for good or for bad. It's in our DNA. But we now know we don't have to lie down and accept this. Our thoughts and practices can affect the way our inherited genes work. It's called *epigenetics*, which simply means "above our genes." Through our attitudes, behaviors, and environments, we can reverse, rise above, and change how our bodies and brains read our DNA sequences.[7]

We are no longer victims of our past. With God's help, we can carve out a new path that promises joy and happiness not only for us but for our family to the fourth generation. Deuteronomy tells us that joy can extend to one thousand generations (7:9–16)! But we must choose to leave the past behind us for true change to take place.

Not being held hostage by your past and living in the present moment with an embedded hope for the future in your mind and heart is most definitely a part of the recipe for joy.

# A DIFFERENT PERSPECTIVE ON FAILURE

Giannis Antetokounmpo is a Greek-Nigerian power forward who plays in the National Basketball Association for the Milwaukee Bucks. The team has won two NBA championships in its history: 1971 and 2021. The Bucks posted the best record of any team in the 2022–2023 season. It certainly looked like a repeat was coming. But it was not to be.

The Bucks' winning streak came to a shocking end when they were eliminated by the eighth seed, the Miami Heat, in the opening round of the NBA playoffs. During the postgame interviews, a reporter asked Giannis: "Do you view this season as a failure?" Giannis placed his oversized hands around his head, sighed, and said the following:

> You asked me the same question last year, Eric. Do you get a promotion every year on your job—no, right?—so every year your work is a failure. Yes or no. No. Every year you work toward something, toward a goal, which is to get a promotion, to be able to take care of your family, to be able to provide a house for them, to take care of your parents. You work toward a goal. It is not a failure. It's a step towards success . . . Michael Jordan played fifteen years. He won six championships. Were the other nine years a failure? That is what you are telling me. It's the wrong question. There is not failure in sports. There are good days, bad days. Some days you are able to be successful; some days you are not. Some days it's your turn; some days it is not your turn. That is what sports is about. You don't always win. Simple as that. You are going to come back next year and try to be better and build good habits, try to play better . . . and hopefully we can win a championship.

Then he wrapped up his comments:

So, fifty years, from 1971–2021, we didn't win a championship. It was fifty years of failure? No, it was not! It was steps to it, and we were able to win one. Hopefully, we can win another one.[8]

This has certainly been the story of my life. I have gone through a few seasons of insane momentum, recognition, and success. And then, everything gets quiet and still. More than that, everything you touch doesn't seem to work at all. You branch out and try new things, implement new ideas, and it doesn't get the lift you expected based on the short season of past success. If you are not careful, you can start believing that your best days are behind you.

But did you know that Thomas Edison failed to invent the light-bulb the first two thousand times he tried? This is what Paul was trying to say to us, but he was talking about more than winning basketball games and creating lightbulbs (as important as these things are). He was talking about the quality of our lives. If we want to increase our joy despite our past, we need to put the past behind us.

## THE JOY CHALLENGE

Dr. Daniel Amen, in his excellent book *You, Happier*, identified what he called the 13 Dragons from the Past.[9] For your Joy Challenge today, I want you to identify which of these thirteen dragons has the greatest hold on you. Circle it, once you've identified it. Then, in your journal, write out a single paragraph to explain your choices. Reflect on why this is an issue for you. Be super honest and specific.

**ABANDONED, INVISIBLE, OR INSIGNIFICANT DRAGON—** feeling alone, unseen, or unimportant

**INFERIOR OR FLAWED DRAGON**—feeling less than others

**ANXIOUS DRAGON**—feeling fearful and overwhelmed

**WOUNDED DRAGON**—feeling bruised by past trauma

**SHOULD AND SHAMING DRAGON**—feeling racked with guilt

**SPECIAL, SPOILED, OR ENTITLED DRAGON**—feeling more
special than others

**RESPONSIBLE DRAGON**—feeling the need to take care of
others

**ANGRY DRAGON**—harboring hurt and rage

**JUDGMENTAL DRAGON**—holding harsh or critical opinions of
others due to past injustices

**DEATH DRAGON**—fearing the future and the lack of a
meaningful life

**GRIEF AND LOSS DRAGON**—feeling loss and fear of loss

**HOPELESS AND HELPLESS DRAGON**—having a pervasive
sense of despair and discouragement

**ANCESTRAL DRAGON**—feeling affected by issues from past
generations

Find a small note card or piece of paper and write out the name and description of the dragon you identify as your main struggle. Place this note card somewhere where you will see it for at least one week (on your bathroom mirror, the dash of your car, your desktop, or by your bedside table). Then pray a simple prayer. Tell God you would really, really like to slay this dragon, but you need his help. Believe me, he can help.

Finally, share this goal with someone else. It can be your spouse, sibling, or a good friend. If you feel comfortable, you can even post about it on your social media platforms and ask people to pray for you.

When you come to the end of the day, write down your reflections on naming this dragon and how you feel about finally putting it to rest in your life.

CARRY YOUR JOY CUBE WITH YOU EVERYWHERE YOU GO TODAY. MAKE SURE YOU POP IT OPEN SO YOU AND OTHERS CAN KEEP THE PRINCIPLES EVER BEFORE YOU. DON'T FORGET TO GO OVER YOUR MEMORY VERSE FOR THIS SECTION: PHILIPPIANS 3:13.

# FOCUS ON THE FUTURE

*Brothers and sisters, I do not consider myself yet to have taken hold of it. But one thing I do: Forgetting what is behind and straining toward what is ahead, I press on toward the goal to win the prize for which God has called me heavenward in Christ Jesus. All of us, then, who are mature should take such a view of things. And if on some point you think differently, that too God will make clear to you. Only let us live up to what we have already attained.*

**–PHILIPPIANS 3:13-16**

Paul introduced us to the last joy principle by focusing in on the "one thing" that drove his life: to obtain full and complete knowledge of Christ (Philippians 3:8). As with any vision, there has to be a strategy to achieve it, and Paul's strategy was twofold. The first part of the strategy was encapsulated in the joy principle from the last chapter and involved putting the past behind us, abandoning our sense of identity from past achievements that were focused on the wrong meaning of success, forgiving ourselves, and accepting God's forgiveness for past mistakes.

Here, Paul addressed the second part of his strategy: focusing on the future. He talked about straining toward what is ahead. The word *straining* in verse 13 is a "graphic word chosen from the athletic arena and pictures the Christian as a runner with his body bent forward, his hands outstretched, his head fixed frontward never giving a backward glance, and his eye fastened on the goal."[1] The runner is stretching every nerve and every muscle. In other words, if we are going to advance in the knowledge of Jesus, it will take intense concentration and effort.

For close to five years, I lived next door to a professional golfer. I watched him strive hard to keep his PGA tour card, to make the weekly cut and dream of one day winning the first-place trophy. When you watch these guys on television, their smooth swings make the whole thing look so effortless. It's not. It is a grind to play with the best in the world.

Finally, he got an amazing break and was able to secure Butch Harmon as his golf coach. Butch only coaches winners or people who become winners when he coaches them. Butch told my neighbor he would win by the end of the year, and sure enough he did. Not just once but six times almost back-to-back! I'll forever remember the night he brought the huge Wanamaker Trophy he'd won at the PGA Championship over to my house and used it as the centerpiece for our dinner. What a memorable moment!

Not long after that major victory, though, he and his wife both got Lyme disease, resulting from a tick bite. There are many side effects to this condition and still no cure. My neighbor's symptoms mirrored those of the flu and came with brain fog. Now he lives with this disease due to no fault of his own. He hasn't won a tournament since, but he also hasn't given up. Both he and his wife hashtag just about all their Instagram posts with the phrase #keepmoving. They can't do anything about the past; the reality is they have Lyme disease now. The only productive thing they can do is to keep pressing forward. Nothing else makes any sense. Recently, though, he has started appearing on the top of the leaderboard again. I just checked, and he made another cut to play this weekend!

I think that is what Paul was talking about here when he said, "I press on toward the goal" (v. 14). There are days when the small tick called *sin* penetrates our skin and gets the best of us. Pursuing the goal of knowing Christ seems elusive then—one step forward, two steps back. But listen to what Paul wrote to the Christians in Rome about this struggle:

> I'm full of myself—after all, I've spent a long time in sin's prison. What I don't understand about myself is that I decide one way, but then I act another, doing things I absolutely despise. (Romans 7:15 MSG)

So, what do you do when you go backward? You get up and you #keepmoving forward toward the goal.

For Paul it wasn't just about winning the race but winning the right race. He was fully focused on taking hold of "the prize for which God has called me heavenward in Christ Jesus" (v. 14). The New American Standard translation uses the phrase "upward call" instead of the word *heavenward*. In the ancient Olympic Games that Paul had in mind here, there were judges who presided over the games called *Hellanodikai*. These highly esteemed officials, perched over the arena, had the distinct pleasure of announcing the winner of the races. They would call the winner up to stand in front of the crowd for all to see. The Hellanodikai would then announce the name of the victor, his father's name, and his country.

Picture our modern-day Olympics where the gold-medal winner is called up to stand on the highest platform as the medal goes around their neck and the national anthem of their country is played. Paul was envisioning the day when his name would be called out by the Divine Hellanodikai (aka God). God, the Judge, calls him up to his elevated chair, announcing Paul as the winner and placing the gold medal around his neck.

Five years after Paul penned this letter, he found himself once again in prison in Rome. This time he wasn't under house arrest but in a dungeon. When he penned his second letter to Timothy from that dungeon, he was perhaps only months away from his execution. Toward the end of the letter, he wrote these words:

> For I am already being poured out like a drink offering, and the time for my departure is near. I have fought the good fight, I have finished the race, I have kept the faith. Now there is in store for me the crown of righteousness, which the Lord, the righteous Judge, will award to me on that day—and not only to me, but also to all who have longed for his appearing. (2 Timothy 4:6–8)

Half a decade later, he was still singularly focused on the prize. He knew he was close. He played the scene over and over again in his mind's eye. The Judge, the Divine Hellanodikai, would call him up and award him with the victor's crown. Everything for Paul was focused on this goal. And now he was commending it to us. Notice in the verse above he said it wasn't just available to him "but also to all who have longed for [Jesus'] appearing."

Let me ask you, Would this bring you joy?

# LOOKING TOWARD THE FINISH LINE

There are at least two reasons why Paul's strategy increases our joy despite our circumstances, other people, and our past. First, it has been proven that people who set goals and are future focused are happier than people who get stuck in the past.

Achieving goals releases dopamine in the brain. Dopamine, you'll remember, is a messenger of pleasure. Dr. John Vervaeke, professor and philosopher at the University of Toronto, said, "There is huge neuropsychological literature that indicates that you experience positive emotion when you see yourself moving towards a valued goal. That's what the dopaminergic tract responds to."[2] That is how God wired our brains.

The top performance coaches will tell you that you get way more momentum focusing on your successes than beating yourself up over your failures. The former is precisely what Paul was doing. He forgot the mistakes of his past and zeroed in on his future. This is what energized him, even while he sat in prison. How did that work? If Paul focused on his past, it would perpetually haunt him. If he dwelled on his current circumstance, it would depress him. Instead, every day he anticipated the achievement of his goal, and it lifted his soul.

In a recent article in the *Atlantic* entitled "Running Faster by Focusing on the Finish Line," Olga Khazan wrote, "People who gaze at an object in the distance go faster and feel less exertion than those who let their attention wander."[3] Paul's attention didn't wander. It was firmly and unwaveringly fixed on a magnificent goal.

But it wasn't just having a goal that brought Paul joy. It was having the right goal of knowing Christ as deeply as he could. Paul took this to another level and "strained" forward to discover his full potential through his relationship with Christ. The finish line for Paul was being called upward into the presence of God, to hear God say his name out loud, to receive his crown of righteousness, and enter into the eternal community with Jesus. The anticipated achievement of that goal shot Paul's joy through the roof.

And remember, he said that this wasn't just something available to him but to all who longed for Christ's appearing. He was recommending this to you and to me.

## THE JOY CHALLENGE

We need to adopt the same future focus as Paul. We need to set our eyes on deepening our relationship with Christ. We need to anticipate the day when God calls us upward and announces our name and gives us a crown of righteousness.

This is a huge goal that can be overwhelming. So, let's go for a series of smaller wins instead. Psychologists tell us that achieving mini goals leading to a bigger goal still completes the reward cycle in our brains that gives us a dopamine hit and increases our pleasure and joy. Follow these steps today to start working on your future focus:

1. **DECLARE:** Tell God you want to adopt Paul's goal of deepening your relationship with him. You can speak this prayer out loud or write it in your journal.

2. **ANTICIPATE:** Imagine and meditate on the day coming when God, the Divine Hellanodikai, will call you to come up to stand before him and, based on your faith in Jesus, place a crown of righteousness on your head and welcome you into his eternal kingdom. Close your eyes and get specific and detailed in this encounter. You can imagine it in your mind or write it out in your journal.

3. **GO FOR A SMALL WIN:** Look for one way you can win today

in deepening your relationship with Christ. If you haven't been to church in a long time, make plans to attend this Sunday. If you are not in a small group with other Christians, take a step toward joining one. Or, read or listen to a chapter from the Gospels, like John 15 or 17. Once you complete this small win, journal your thoughts.

CARRY YOUR JOY CUBE WITH YOU EVERYWHERE YOU GO TODAY. MAKE SURE YOU POP IT OPEN SO YOU AND OTHERS CAN KEEP THE PRINCIPLES EVER BEFORE YOU. DON'T FORGET TO GO OVER YOUR MEMORY VERSE FOR THIS SECTION: PHILIPPIANS 3:13.

# SURROUND YOURSELF WITH THE RIGHT PEOPLE

*Join together in following my example, brothers and sisters, and just as you have us as a model, keep your eyes on those who live as we do. For, as I have often told you before and now tell you again even with tears, many live as enemies of the cross of Christ. Their destiny is destruction, their god is their stomach, and their glory is in their shame. Their mind is set on earthly things. But our citizenship is in heaven. And we eagerly await a Savior from there, the Lord Jesus Christ, who, by the power that enables him to bring everything under his control, will transform our lowly bodies so that they will be like his glorious body.*

**–PHILIPPIANS 3:17-21**

The late Dr. John Walvoord, president of the seminary I graduated from, wrote, "Although chapter three of Philippians is largely a digression after the initial exhortation to rejoice (3:1), nevertheless, it indirectly provides many causes for rejoicing."[1] I agree! In this chapter, Paul already gave us four power-packed principles to increase our joy despite our past:

- Stay clear of legalism (3:1–6).
- Recalculate what really matters (3:7–11).
- Put your past behind you (3:13).
- Focus on the future (3:13–16).

If applied habitually, these principles for living will give you cause to rejoice—guaranteed! The final principle in this chapter promises the same as it exhorts us to surround ourselves with the right people.

Many people experience low places in their life, but not because they lack talent or intelligence. They live in a place of disappointment and discouragement because they spent too many years hanging around the wrong people—people who caused them to waste their time and lower their sights; people who have led them down dead-end streets and senseless roundabouts. Paul cut it straight in this section of his letter and invited us to make a change. He did the same for the followers of Jesus in the city of Corinth: "Do not be misled: 'Bad company corrupts good character'" (1 Corinthians 15:33). If this is you, it is time to put your past behind you and set your sights on some people who can inspire you to new heights and greater joy.

Paul opened by calling the Philippian believers to follow his example. He was not being arrogant here, as though he had his life all figured out. He just admitted a few verses ago that he didn't. But Paul was their spiritual father, as he was to many people he ministered to. Expectedly, he was further along in his journey with Jesus than those he pastored. For you Star Wars fans, Paul was like Yoda. Yoda was further along than Luke Skywalker and sought to pass his knowledge and wisdom to him. Paul wasn't any more arrogant than the soft-spoken Jedi. Life's hard lessons have a way of stripping us of our pride. A person who is full of wisdom is a person who got there on the path of humility. This is definitely Paul's story.

Paul was not asking for blind obedience here—to the contrary. His offer was conditional: *If* you see me following the life principles of Jesus, *then* follow me. *If* you don't see me following the life principles of Jesus, *then* don't follow me.

Paul knew his distance from the Philippians would make it more difficult to follow his daily example, so he expanded the pool of candidates by instructing them to "keep your eyes on those who live as we do" (v. 17). Notice he didn't instruct them to listen to their teaching but to keep their eyes on how they live. The Christian life is more caught than taught. The same word Paul used to describe how the runner should keep his eyes fixed on the goal marker he now used here to describe the intensity by which we should watch the lives of these spiritual Jedi mentors.

This is not the only place in the Bible that offers this precept. The wonderful book of Psalms opens with this admonition:

> Oh, the joys of those who do not
> follow the advice of the wicked,
> or stand around with sinners,
> or join in with mockers.
>
> **(1:1 NLT)**

You want joy? Be mindful of who you hang with! For one thing, a positive mentor is going to show you, primarily by their life, how to live out these twenty principles on increasing your joy. When it comes to a subject as important as joy, who wants to go it alone and engage in the frustrating dance of trial and error? I know I don't. So, let us be mindful to hang out with people ahead of us on the journey who can show us the way.

Paul then spent a little time on the people the Philippians should avoid. His language was straightforward and a bit unconventional for a preacher, as it also was earlier in the chapter. Instead of calling out those who were taking the people he deeply loved down a destructive path, he called out their modus operandi and registered it with rhetoric:

- They live as enemies of the cross.
- Their destiny is their destruction.
- Their god is their stomach.
- Their glory is in their shame.
- Their minds are set on earthly things.

Who were these people? Scholars have debated this question and have narrowed it to two possible groups. They might be the same Jewish folks Paul addressed at the opening of the chapter, those who invaded the church. They denied the role of the death of Jesus on the cross for the forgiveness of sins. This is bedrock to the gospel message and the possession of eternal life. That is why their destiny was their destruction. They observed the Old Testament dietary laws and made conformity to these laws a requirement for salvation, thus "their god is their stomach." As we have seen before, they made circumcision another requirement for salvation, so he said their "glory is in their shame." New Testament scholar Gerald Hawthorne wrote, "Shame is more likely to be a reference to 'nakedness,' one's private parts"[2] that should be unpresentable, but these guys were flaunting them for everyone to see. I know—a bit graphic. Then he finished by telling us their minds were set on earthly things. Dr. Hawthorne brought it all together:

These people have permitted food laws and the rite of circumcision to become gods to them. They have become so preoccupied with scrupulous observance of ritual detail, so obsessed with the supreme importance of circumcision and with seeing that it was carried out and carried out correctly, that they had no thought for anything or anyone higher. God became obscured by religion. The true God was replaced by a false god to whom devotion was duly paid.[3]

Another group Paul might have been roasting here were people who believed that matter is evil and can never be holy. In their thinking, since the body is matter, it is evil and has no chance of being redeemed. Therefore, engaging in any activity with the body was okay, and it didn't matter. Now, it takes some fancy footwork to get there, but you can imagine how attractive this point of view was. You can eat, drink, and party as much as you want with no spiritual consequences—"their god is their stomach." You can engage in any type of sexual activity, and it's quite all right and even encouraged—"their glory is in their shame" (v. 19).

Whatever the identity of these people, it tore Paul up that they lived this way and made the decision to do so. He didn't want the Philippians hanging around them and potentially being persuaded to go in that direction. Getting sucked into either one of these rabbit holes would, as the psalmist said, "rob you of joy!"

Paul finished by reminding the believers that their "citizenship is in heaven" (v. 20). The Philippians would have understood this better than most of us. Philippi was a Roman colony. As a benefit, they possessed full rights as Roman citizens, even though they were living in a foreign land. In return, they were expected to adopt the ways of Rome. Paul's point, then, was that every local church is a colony of heaven. Its members enjoy the full benefits of citizenship of the heavenly city, even though they live in a distant land. Yet, we are charged with the responsibility for living our lives according to the vision and values of the country listed on our spiritual passports (heaven). We do not allow the environment we live in on earth to determine the quality of our behavior. That's the point.

Paul reminded us that our destination is not destruction but rather eternal life in the heavenly city. One day, Jesus will return and take us to our homeland where our frail, disease-prone bodies will be transformed into the same kind of body Jesus received at his resurrection: imperishable! Certainly, this declaration of hope will heighten your happiness in spite of your circumstances, other people, or your past.

## OUR PROPENSITY TOWARD MIMICRY

When Paul invited us to follow him, he used the Greek word *mimitai*, where we get our English word *mimic*. Humans are designed by God as mimickers. It is one of the primary ways we learn.

Social work researchers Karen Gerdes and Elizabeth Segal pass on some great insights on how our brain is wired:

We now know through the work of neuroscientists that the human brain is wired to mimic other people, and this mimicry involves actual involuntary, physiological experience in the observer. Human beings tend to imitate actions that they see. Physiologically, our brains include mirror neurons, which react to actions that are seen as if we are doing the action ourselves. It is largely an unconscious and automatic experience. When we hear people speak, observe their vocal nuances, watch their posture, gestures, and facial expressions, etc., neural networks in our brains are stimulated by the "shared representations," generating feelings within us that reflect the experience of those we are observing.[4]

So, we will have an almost involuntary propensity to mimic the people we hang around. If you hang around people whose paths are destructive, you will likely be heading there yourself, whether you are willing to admit it or not. If you hang around people who lead productive and fruitful lives filled with joy and constructive, God-honoring outcomes, well, that is where you will likely end up. Simply ask yourself, "Where do I want to end up?"

## HONEST JOHN, LAMPWICK, AND JIMINY CRICKET

In 1940, Disney released its second full-length animation, *Pinocchio*. This heartwarming story, based on Carlo Collodi's 1883 children's novel, does a wonderful job of illustrating the importance of hanging around the right people.

The story begins with a woodcarver in Italy named Geppetto who carves a wooden puppet and "wishes upon a star" that the puppet would be a real boy, the son he never had. A blue fairy visits Geppetto's home and brings Pinocchio to life, telling him he can become a real boy if he proves himself to be brave, truthful, and unselfish. Then, we are introduced to Jiminy Cricket—yes, a cricket in real life—who is assigned to play the role of Pinocchio's conscience, trying to lead him to make good choices. Geppetto is ecstatic.

The next morning, on the way to school, Pinocchio meets a con-artist fox, Honest John, who convinces Pinocchio to join Stromboli's puppet show. Pinocchio agrees and starts hanging with this new community of shady characters. Quickly Pinocchio becomes the star attraction, but when he tries to leave to go home, Stromboli locks him in a birdcage and takes him on a road tour. When the blue fairy appears on the scene, Pinocchio lies about what has happened and his nose grows. The marionette is digging himself deeper into trouble.

It turns out Honest John has been hired to find disobedient boys to take a vacation to Pleasure Island. Pinocchio now qualifies. Here Pinocchio starts hanging out with another delinquent boy named Lampwick. There are no rules on Pleasure Island, and before you know it, Pinocchio has joined in with a team of boys engaging in vices like drinking and smoking. No one knows there is a curse on Pleasure Island that transforms disobedient boys into donkeys who are, in turn, sold as slaves. Pinocchio witnesses his friend Lampwick's transformation into the hoofed mammal and his anxiety skyrockets. With the help of Jiminy Cricket, Pinocchio escapes with only donkey ears and a tail.

When Pinocchio and Jiminy return home, they discover that Geppetto took off to Pleasure Island to rescue his son from this nightmare. Upon finding that Pinocchio was not there, he gets back into his boat to head home but ends up swallowed by Monstro, a giant sperm whale. Determined to rescue his father, Pinocchio, with Jiminy by his side, finds a way to get swallowed by Monstro as well, reuniting with Geppetto. Then Pinocchio devises a scheme to get Monstro to sneeze them out—and it works. Once they are outside of the grand mammal, the angry Monstro smashes their small wooden raft with his tail. Pinocchio selflessly pulls his dad to safety just as Monstro crashes into the raft, seemingly killing Pinocchio. But because Pinocchio proved himself to be brave, truthful, and unselfish, the blue fairy revives him and turns him into a real boy. And they live happily ever after.

I remember how mesmerized I was as I watched this movie as a little boy. It is a fictional story that carries a great nonfictional punch for children and adults alike, reminding us that the outcome of our lives depends on surrounding ourselves with the right people.

# THE JOY CHALLENGE

Here is your Joy Challenge for today, as you consider the people you're surrounding yourself with. Start by doing some reflection and journaling, in response to the following questions:

- Who are the groups of people with whom you surround yourself?
- Are these people leading you in the right direction or tempting you toward Pleasure Island?
- Are there some groups of people you need to stop hanging around because their values are pulling you in the wrong direction? Are you prepared to move away from this group?
- Who is your Paul? Who is a mentor whose life provides a good model for you to mimic?

If you are fortunate to have one or more Pauls in your life, contact them today to thank them for providing you with such a strong role model to follow. If you don't have a Paul, this becomes a challenge that might take you more time than just today. Ponder the names of people who might be able to fill that role in your life. Pray about it and consider scheduling some time with them. You are not really asking them to mentor you unless they have the time. You are simply seeking to organically hang in the same circles as they do. Ask them if you might be able to reach out from time to time to get counsel on a decision you are facing.

Now, consider whether you are a Paul for someone else. Ponder who might look to you in this way. Write down their names. Start with one of the names on your list. Are you mindful that this person is watching how you are living, treating people, and making decisions? Does this compel you to make any changes in the habits and patterns of your life? Journal your thoughts.

REMEMBER TO CARRY YOUR JOY CUBE WITH YOU EVERYWHERE YOU GO TODAY. MAKE SURE YOU POP IT OPEN SO YOU AND OTHERS CAN KEEP THE PRINCIPLES EVER BEFORE YOU. DON'T FORGET TO GO OVER YOUR MEMORY VERSE FOR THIS SECTION (PHILIPPIANS 3:13), AND ALSO REHEARSE ALL THE VERSES YOU HAVE LEARNED SO FAR.

# PART 4

# JOY THAT
# DEFEATS WORRY

### MEMORY VERSES

*Do not be anxious about anything, but in every situation, by prayer and petition, with thanksgiving, present your requests to God. And the peace of God, which transcends all understanding, will guard your hearts and your minds in Christ Jesus.*

**–PHILIPPIANS 4:6-7**

When I was a kid growing up in the urban core of Cleveland, Ohio, we would daily head to the neighborhood sandlot for a game of pickup baseball. One day, when I was eight years old, I ventured there with my best friend, Joseph.

On that particular day, there was no one at the lot except two older kids we had never seen before. The boys presented us with a game, a wager. For every ball they hit over the fence, we would give them fifty cents. For every ball we hit over the fence, they would give us five dollars. The spread was huge, and we gladly accepted before they changed their minds. I immediately started dreaming of all the things I could buy with five . . . ten . . . fifteen dollars. Back in 1969, that was a lot of money. Only problem was, neither one of us had ever hit a ball over the fence. What could possibly go wrong?

We agreed we would play three rounds. In each round, both teams had ten tries to get the ball over the fence. We went first. After ten attempts, as expected, we had no balls over the fence. Now it was their turn. Of their ten tries, they got six balls over the fence. On our second round, we were zero for ten. On their second attempt, they put seven balls over the fence. On our third round, we got close but no cigar. Zero for thirty. On their third round, they racked up seven more home runs. They were twenty for thirty.

I'll do the math for you, so you don't have to. We were down ten dollars, or five dollars each. I didn't have five dollars. What was I going to do? I told our opponents that I needed to go home and get the money. "Wait here and I will be right back," I said. I had no intention of coming back. Since they weren't from the neighborhood, they had no idea where I lived. It was the best plan I could conjure up under duress.

I jumped the fence and headed home. When I got home, my parents were sitting on the front porch drinking sweet tea. They asked me how I was doing. I said, "Fine." But I wasn't fine. I was freaking out. I went into my bedroom and shut the door.

I didn't have a next move—nothing. This was as far as my plan took me. I pondered all my options and came up with none. This was it for me. I would spend the rest of my life quarantined in my bedroom ruminating on just how stupid it was for me to enter into such a bet. What made me think I would be able to magically hit a ball over the fence when I had not done it once, not ever? Greed had gotten the best of me. I looked in the mirror and could see my accelerated heart rate beating in the veins of my neck. My life as I knew it was over. I was overcome in an avalanche of anxiety, drowning in a deluge of discouragement, wiped out in a whirlwind of worry. This incident was rooted in a poor decision I made. But I have come to discover, in my six decades of living, that worry and anxiety have many origins besides our own stupidity.

Worry. Ever do any of that? You certainly wouldn't be alone. It is a human condition. Current statistics show that 60 percent of Americans worry every day.[1] I think someone is not telling the truth. My guess is that it's closer to 90 percent.

What are the top five things we worry about?[2] Here they are in order:

1. **MONEY:** Even people who have money worry about money. Once you make it, you have to find a way to hold on to it or you will go backward. This is a constant source of anxiety, even for the rich.

2. **THE FUTURE:** As Homo sapiens, we have more brain power than the other creatures on land and in the sea, but we can only see so far ahead. We can't see around the bend. We don't know when the other shoe is going to drop. So, we fret about it.

3. **JOB SECURITY:** We work hard to get the right job, and then we worry about keeping it. We live in a dog-eat-dog world. The golden rule of the workplace: "Do one unto others, before they do one unto you."

4. **RELATIONSHIPS:** It takes two to make a good relationship. *How can I count on the other person to do the right thing by me? How can I have the wisdom and fortitude to do the right thing by them?* Yikes, the chances are good this is not going to work out. Let's get our worry on.

5. **HEALTH:** My mom passed away of pancreatic cancer at the age of sixty-two. It all started with what appeared to be an innocent cough. For years after my mom passed, whenever I got a cough or any kind of minor ache, I immediately assumed it was cancer. It occupied my mind 24-7.

How many times have you woken up at three in the morning and taken a head dive into a pool of worry and anxiety about the way things are, the stuff you have to do, something you forgot, your frustration with someone else? You can literally think the world is coming to an end. Then, when you get up later in the morning, you realize the issue wasn't that big of a deal. The sky, as it turns out, is not falling. There is a perfectly good explanation for why this happens.

Around three or four in the morning, our neurobiology reaches a turning point. Greg Murray, professor and director of the Centre for Mental Health at Swinburne University of Technology, explained what happens: "Core body temperature starts to rise, sleep drive is reducing (we have already had a chunk of sleep), secretion of melatonin (the sleep hormone) has peaked, and levels of cortisol (the stress hormone) are increasing as the body prepares to launch us into the day."[3] Even with that explanation, we can't seem to stop ourselves from engaging in the nocturnal dance. Two nights later, we are at it again.

Here's the kicker. Only 8 percent of the stuff we worry about comes true.[4] You have likely heard that statistic before, but has it reduced your worry quota? I'm not pointing the finger at you; I struggle with this myself. I sometimes feel if I worry about it, maybe it won't happen.

Paul had a great deal to worry about. For one, he was in prison and possibly facing execution. More than 8 percent of the things he could have worried about came true. He was executed. Yet, Paul seemed to have a handle on worry, and now he wanted to pass on the secrets to us.

As we finish our last five principles for increasing our joy, we will look at Paul's Holy Spirit–inspired principles to defeat worry in our lives. He addressed the big five just mentioned: our finances, our future, our relationships, our jobs, and our health.

You are almost there. Don't stop now. Frankly, we have saved some of the best for last—or better yet, Paul did. Many psychologists and neurologists agree that one of the principles Paul presented in chapter 4 of Philippians is the single greatest way to win over fear and worry and experience joy and happiness. You'll have to keep going to find out which one it is.

So, how did my boyhood predicament turn out?

I was sequestered in my bedroom for what felt like hours. It was likely just an hour. I believe that was the day I started biting my nails. There was no way out that I could see. I started to ponder who my pallbearers would be.

Then there was a knock at the door. It was my dad. He asked, "Son, did you make a bet with a couple of boys down at the sandlot?" Apparently, the boys asked around and found out where I lived. I so badly wanted to deny this; it was so embarrassing. But in that moment, I said, "Yes, sir." I confessed; I came clean. That alone made me feel better, but I had no idea what was coming next.

He said, "Randall, you never make a bet you can't keep. You got that?" "Yes, sir," I replied, "I will never, never do that again." Then he said words I will never forget: "Son, I paid your debt." My eyes got bigger than a pair of grapefruits. "So, are the boys are gone?" I asked. "Yes, son, they are gone." I ran and gave my dad a hug like never before and exited the bedroom like I had just been released from San Quentin.

As I look back on that situation, I have two major regrets. One, that I agreed to make the bet in the first place. I kept my promise and have never done that again. Second, I wished I had gone to my dad right away. I could have avoided an hour of sheer terror.

News flash: This is the major focus for Paul in this final chapter. He encouraged us to go to God as the primary way of defeating worry in our lives. So, buckle up and get ready for five more life-changing principles that promise to lift your joy.

Before you close the book for the day, though, spend some time reflecting. Record your thoughts in your journal using these prompts:

- What causes you to worry? Is it money, the future, your job, relationships, your health, or something else? Maybe it is more than one thing.
- What is the probability that what you are worrying about is actually going to happen? Is it one of these 8 percents that is likely to happen, or does it possibly fall in the 92 percent category?
- What do you think your life would look like if you could eliminate most of the worry?

If you are up for it, talk this over with someone else and let them share their thoughts. This would be a good conversation to have with the person or group of people who are participating in this challenge with you.

CARRY YOUR JOY CUBE WITH YOU EVERYWHERE YOU GO TODAY. MAKE SURE YOU POP IT OPEN SO YOU AND OTHERS CAN KEEP THE PRINCIPLES EVER BEFORE YOU. GO AHEAD AND START MEMORIZING THE FINAL VERSES IN THIS CHALLENGE: PHILIPPIANS 4:6-7.

PRINCIPLE #16

# SEEK RECONCILIATION IN YOUR RELATIONSHIPS

*Therefore, my brothers and sisters, you whom I love and long for, my joy and crown, stand firm in the Lord in this way, dear friends!*

*I plead with Euodia and I plead with Syntyche to be of the same mind in the Lord. Yes, and I ask you, my true companion, help these women since they have contended at my side in the cause of the gospel, along with Clement and the rest of my co-workers, whose names are in the book of life.*

—PHILIPPIANS 4:1-3

In these first three verses of chapter 4, Paul did something that needed to be done but few people like doing. He confronted two ladies in the church who were at odds with each other. This division was creating tension within the fellowship. Tension in our relationships robs us of joy. That's why our next joy principle is about seeking reconciliation in our relationships.

But before he jumped into the matter at hand, Paul reminded the Philippian believers just how much joy they bring him. He commended them before he commanded them to get their act together. This is a smart strategy for us to apply. Relationship experts tell us we need to make five positive deposits in a relationship for every one withdrawal. Five encouraging comments set you up to dish out one constructive criticism. This confrontation was not a negative. It was meant to be an expression of tough love that guided these women and the entire congregation back to a place of peace. Let's take a look at how Paul affirmed them and set a foundation of love before he confronted them:

- He called them "brothers and sisters" and reminded them they are family.
- He added "whom I love," which is what God the Father said about Jesus at his baptism: "This is my Son, whom I love" (Matthew 3:17).
- Next, he said he "longs for them," voicing a strong yearning to see them again. People love to be longed for.
- Then he used that word we have come to expect in this little letter. He called them "my joy." They not only brought Paul joy, but they were his joy. It was that sparkle in Paul's eye that said, "I am happy with you."
- Lastly, he called them his "crown." This is a garland placed on the head of a guest at a banquet or the victor's wreath presented by the judges to the winner in the Olympic Games. Paul was proud of these people, and he let them know with such heartfelt language.

With five affirmations laid out in succession, he was prepared to present the challenge. There were two ladies in the church fellowship, Euodia and Syntyche, who were at odds with each other. This no doubt was calling for people to take sides, creating a ripple of resentment throughout the fellowship. Interestingly, we are not told what they were fighting about. That probably means this was not a matter of right and wrong but a disagreement over preferences. How true is this in our relationships?

On numerous occasions, particularly in the younger years of our marriage, Rozanne and I would have a pretty intense fight. Two weeks later, we'd be sharing with some close friends that we had a tiff and, for the life of us, we couldn't remember what the core issue had been. Nonetheless, that tension robbed us of a day of joy and no doubt spilled over into the anxiety of our four children.

Here's the sad part for Euodia and Syntyche: This letter was read over and over again in the assembly. You can just feel them cringing as the reader rounds the corner on chapter three and is about to dive into chapter four. "Here we go again, displaying our dirty laundry for all to see," they whisper under their breath. For crying out loud, this letter is in the Bible. We are reading about their fight right now, almost two thousand years later. When we get to heaven and meet them, we will say, "Oh, you are Euodia and Syntyche! We read about you. What was that bee in your bonnet all about anyway?" Hopefully, under these circumstances, they might get a chuckle out of it. It might cause us to think twice if we knew our tiffs with one another were going to be recorded in an eternal book for everyone to read forever!

Paul then pleaded with the congregation, who were closer to the situation, to join in to help these ladies reconcile. Reconciliation, Paul was showing us, is a communal effort. Too often we stand on the sidelines and watch two people go after it and we say nothing, or we take a side, which complicates the argument and expands it. That is not how a Christian family should function. This is not how a Christian church should function. The ones who are fighting are harming their relationship and creating tension that robs them of joy. Their conflict is like the loss of cabin pressure in an airplane at thirty thousand feet. It sucks the joy oxygen out of the room. It's unacceptable for followers of Jesus.

Paul was trying to preserve the unity of their fellowship. These weren't bad women. They had just lost their way or let pride come between them. He complimented the ladies, sharing that "they have contended at my side in the cause of the gospel" (v. 3). I think it is important to note that even good people fight and disagree with one another from time to time. Since we, like Paul, haven't attained full maturity in the Christian life (3:12), we are going to experience a few setbacks along the way. It is unrealistic to think we will never have conflict. The number and frequency should reduce as we grow older and grow up in Christ, but likely they will never be completely eliminated from our family or community. The key is addressing it right away before things get out of hand.

Paul ended verse 3, reminding the church that Euodia's and Syntyche's names are written in the "book of life." This is a book referred to throughout the Bible and contains the names of all the people who are citizens in the eternal kingdom following the return of Jesus.[1] This is a register of God's covenant people. I think Paul added this to remind us of two things:

1. If God can forgive us of everything we have ever done and still grant us access into his kingdom forever, certainly we can forgive one another for this one struggle.
2. We are going to be spending eternity together. We should probably start learning how to get along now.

You want to increase your joy and defeat worry in your life? Seek reconciliation in your relationships!

# THE PEACE OF FORGIVENESS
# AND RECONCILIATION

Someone wisely said, "Not forgiving someone else is like drinking poison and expecting the other person to die." This is so true. I've personally experienced the poison running through my veins—not worth it. The opposite is also true. Forgiving someone is like drinking medicine and expecting the other person to be healed—worth it.

Dr. Dan Baker, in his wonderful book *What Happy People Know*, gave us the straight scoop on the toll unreconciled relationships take on our lives, health, and joy.

From a medical perspective, hate is a heavy burden, creating chronic overstimulation of the sympathetic nervous system, which contributes strongly to depressed immunity, insomnia, hypertension, muscle pain, colitis, ulcers, heart attack, stroke, memory loss, migraines, and impaired cognitive function. But the worst damage is to peace of mind. It's impossible to hate and be happy at the same time.[2]

Simply put, hate is a joy robber for you and everyone in striking distance of your melodrama. Baker agreed with Jesus: "The important thing is just to get the hate out of your heart"[3] (Matthew 15:18–19).

Dr. Daniel Amen looked at the flip side, the positive side, of this phenomenon:

A wealth of research points to healthy relationships as the greatest predictor of a happy life. Brain imaging studies show that strengthening relationships can actually improve brain function in people with depression. By enhancing your relationships, you can optimize your brain and increase your happiness.[4]

Having healthy relationships where we are at peace with one another is perhaps more vital to our joy quotient than we knew. As I have said before, peace and joy are cousins. One comes out of the other. So how do we go about cultivating this kind of peace and increasing our joy? One way is through reconciliation.

Reconciliation is not always about forgiveness. In many cases it is about realizing we were the one who was wrong, or we were the one who put too much importance on being right over the relationship. In most cases, the topic at hand is seldom more important than damaging a relationship. Now, sometimes it is—just not most of the time. Most of us need to learn the fine art of agreeing to disagree. And a huge part of that comes down to humility.

Over my six decades of life (five of them as a follower of Jesus), I have found humility to be the virtue that most helps me keep peace in my relationships and most helps me in the reconciliation process. Remember Philippians 2:3–4: "Do nothing out of selfish ambition or vain conceit. Rather, in humility value others above yourselves, not looking to your own interests but each of you to the interests of others." You can take that advice to the relationship bank.

## THE LONG JOURNEY OF RECONCILIATION

*The Straight Story* is a biographical drama based on the true story of Alvin Straight, an elderly World War II vet, and his most unusual journey to reconcile with his estranged brother, Lyle.[5] When Alvin hears that Lyle has suffered a stroke, Alvin makes up his mind to visit Lyle and hopefully make amends before he dies. Because his eyes and legs are weak, Alvin doesn't have a driver's license. So, he decides to hitch a trailer to his thirty-year-old John Deere tractor—maximum speed: five miles per hour. He sets off on the 240-mile journey from

Laurens, Iowa, to Mount Zion, Wisconsin. What could possibly go wrong?

Alvin's first attempt fails when the old motor breaks down and he is forced to haul the tractor back home. He purchases a used transmission from 1966 that is still intact and takes off again toward his mission of reconciling with Lyle. As he continues on his journey, Alvin meets one difficulty after another. He starts running short on food along the way, but then he meets a distraught woman who has hit a deer, and she gives him meat to cook for dinner. Then, as he is riding down a steep hill, his brakes fail. The tractor is speeding out of control, but he manages to come to a stop. It is here he discovers his mower has transmission problems. Running low on cash, he phones his daughter and asks her to send him his Social Security check. As his tractor is getting fixed, he is invited into town for a drink by a fellow war veteran. Alvin orders a glass of milk, and the two exchange stories of fighting against the Germans in World War II.

Back on the road again, Alvin crosses the Mississippi River and makes camp at a cemetery. There, he chats with a priest who knows his brother Lyle. The priest tells Alvin that Lyle never mentioned he had a brother. Alvin says to the priest, "Whatever it was that made me and Lyle so mad, it don't matter anymore. I wanna make peace. I want to sit with him, look up at the stars like we used to so long ago."

Alvin finally makes it to Mount Zion, but his tractor stops just a few miles from Lyle's house. A farmer with a large tractor stops by and helps Alvin get the tractor running again and leads him to his brother's house.

When he arrives, he finds it dilapidated. He calls out for his brother, who appears at the door with the aid of a walker. With the assistance of his two canes, Alvin makes his way to the door. Lyle invites Alvin to sit down on the porch. With tears rolling down his face, Lyle looks at Alvin's mower-tractor contraption and asks if Alvin did all this just to see him. Alvin simply responds, "I did, Lyle." They spend the evening together on the porch, looking up at the stars like they did so long ago.

There's something incredibly moving about simple stories like this. Why is that? I think it's because we know deep down inside the importance of reconciliation in relationships. Alvin went to great lengths to make things right with his brother. And, in the end, that encounter on Lyle's porch must have brought an enormous amount of joy to both men.

Jesus said, "Therefore, if you are offering your gift at the altar and there remember that your brother or sister has something against you, leave your gift there in front of the altar. First go and be reconciled to them; then come and offer your gift" (Matthew 5:23–25). If we want to live a life of joy and rightness with God, we must first humble ourselves and make things right with one another.

## THE JOY CHALLENGE

Today's Joy Challenge is just that—a challenge. I want you to begin by taking a little inventory. Is there any relationship in your life that needs to be reconciled? Write down the name or names of the people you need to reconcile with in your journal.

What is the nature of the conflict? Are they angry with you for something you did, or are you angry with them for something they did? Or is it that you just can't get along or see eye to eye?

What is holding you back from making the first move toward reconciliation? Is it fear, stubbornness, unforgiveness, unwillingness—on your part or on their part? It is very possible that the other person is simply unwilling to let go of whatever happened in the past, but you may be surprised. Alvin certainly thought that might be the case with

Lyle, but it didn't stop him from trying. As it was with Alvin and Lyle or with Euodia and Syntyche, reconciliation can bring a deep sense of relief and joy as you finally let things go.

Do you think this is something Jesus is wanting you to do? Then, maybe today is the day you stop drinking the poison, hoping the other person will die. Your challenge is to first pray and then take your first step toward reconciliation. It could be a phone call, a letter, or perhaps tuning up your riding mower for a personal visit.

For some of you, it is possible that all your relationships are intact and healthy, as far as you know. That is where I currently am, thank God. It is the only way to live. Your challenge, then, is to be the true champion Paul talked about in our passage. Be the one that helps the Euodia and Syntyche in your life to reunite. In your journal, identify who the people are, ask God to help you, and then identify your first step and do it.

Warning: this is not for the faint of heart. But it is the right thing to do. You may fail, but you will have proven to be a good friend or brother or sister. Who knows? You may succeed in igniting restoration in the lives of real people. Wouldn't that be something?

> REMEMBER TO CARRY YOUR JOY CUBE WITH YOU EVERYWHERE YOU GO TODAY. MAKE SURE YOU POP IT OPEN SO YOU AND OTHERS CAN KEEP THE PRINCIPLES EVER BEFORE YOU. KEEP MEMORIZING PHILIPPIANS 4:6-7.

# GIVE WHAT TROUBLES YOU TO GOD

*Rejoice in the Lord always. I will say it again: Rejoice! Let your gentleness be evident to all. The Lord is near. Do not be anxious about anything, but in every situation, by prayer and petition, with thanksgiving, present your requests to God. And the peace of God, which transcends all understanding, will guard your hearts and your minds in Christ Jesus.*

**–PHILIPPIANS 4:4-7**

Hold on to your seats, because psychologists believe what Paul recommended in this principle, and the one he presented in the next chapter, may be the greatest antidotes to fear and worry. After studying the topic of joy for the past five years, reading everything

I can get my hands on, I believe what Paul presented in Philippians 4:6–9 may be the best and most potent advice ever written about how to increase our joy regardless of our circumstances, people, or our past. It will defy our worries.

After addressing the conflict between the two women in the church, Paul was back at it again. He invited us to rejoice not once but twice! Paul was emphasizing through intense repetition, "You really need to get good at this!" And this is not a generic brand of glad making but, rather, is targeted around our relationship with God. He told us to "rejoice in the Lord." The activity is rejoicing. The reason we can be confident of its efficacy is because it is anchored in the trustworthiness of God.

Then Paul invited us to make sure our gentleness is evident to everyone. I think he still had the conflict between Euodia and Syntyche on his mind. Of the three words available in the Greek, Paul chose a word that could be translated "magnanimity" or "sweet reasonableness." Merriam-Webster says it's a "loftiness of spirit enabling one to bear trouble calmly, and to disdain meanness and pettiness, and to display a noble generosity."[1] Lawrence Richards wrote, "Rather than hotly demanding his or her rights, whatever the cost to others, a person with this trait seeks peace in a calm way."[2] This advice will not only aid the two women in their reconciliation but will promote a less stressful environment, which will increase everyone's joy.

To jazz up the invitation, Paul threw in this sentence: "The Lord is near" (v. 5). This is either a reference to space or time or both. If it references space, it means that the Lord is close to us right now, which he is, so we need to be mindful of how we are acting. If it references time, it is referring to the imminent return of Jesus to the earth. Jesus can come back at any moment to judge and to finalize the full benefits of our salvation. We don't want to be caught being a jerk when he arrives. Since both options are true, I think he had both in mind. Seeing Jesus face-to-face should motivate us all.

Now for the crème-de-la-crème advice. In verse 6, Paul made this outlandish command: "Do not be anxious about anything." The Greek word for "anxious" means "to be pulled in different directions." Our hopes pull us in one direction; our fears pull us in the opposite direction. And we are pulled apart![3] Interestingly, the Old English root from where we get the word *worry*, which we perhaps use more than the word *anxious*, means "to strangle." Worry strangles the life out of us. In fact, worry has definite physical consequences: headaches, neck pains, ulcers, even back pains. Worry affects our thinking, our digestion, and even our coordination.[4]

Paul and the Philippians had ample reason for anxiety. Paul was in prison, and the Philippians were constantly facing persecution. They certainly needed to do the things they could do within their control to help the situation. This is a healthy worry or, better, a healthy concern. But Paul and the Philippians and now we are invited not to push that concern into a debilitating anxiety that pulls us in a direction the opposite of our hope in Christ. Paul was not making light of the troubles we face. He was inviting us to rid ourselves of the stranglehold of worry because he was confident that God is greater than all of our troubles. Thus, our next joy principle is to give what troubles us to God.

This is why Paul's single aim was to get to know Christ better. The more you know Christ, the grander your confidence becomes that he is greater than our greatest fear. So, what is the alternative to worry? The simple answer: prayer.

The way to be anxious for nothing is to be prayerful about everything. Prayer is a conversation, a plea, a request, all given to a person, in this case the supreme person of the universe who can hear, know, understand, care about, and respond to the concerns that otherwise would sink us in despair.[5] God already knows what is troubling us, but he wants us to speak it to him.

On several occasions in the Gospels, Jesus asked a person, "What do you want me to do for you?" One particular story involved a blind man who called out to Jesus as he made his way into Jerusalem. The man's need was obvious, but Jesus wanted him to say it out loud. Bartimaeus replied, "Rabbi, I want to see" (Mark 10:46–52). God is inviting us to do the very same thing. To ask him. To speak to him about our needs. Yet, coupled with our prayers, petitions, and requests, he also wants us to add thanksgiving.

This is the key! Did you hear me? This is the key! Karl Barth eloquently wrote, "We begin by praising God for the fact that in this situation, as it is, he is so mightily God. Such a beginning is the end of anxiety."[6] This is precisely mirrored in how Jesus taught the disciples to pray:

> "Our Father in heaven,
> hallowed be your name,
> your kingdom come,
> your will be done,
> on earth as it is in heaven."
>
> **(MATTHEW 6:9-10)**

We begin every prayer by acknowledging that God is high above our problems, and we want him to bring his will from heaven directly to bear on any problem we face on earth. After we have done that, then we pray, "Give us this day our daily bread." Now we are prepared to tell him what is troubling us. "God, we are hungry, and we don't know where our next meal is coming from."

We also need to share with God what we are thankful for in the midst of our request. For example, if you are praying for a child who is struggling in school, you can first thank God that you have a child. If you have a doctor's appointment and you are anxious about the outcome, first thank God for the good health you have enjoyed before this. If you are worried about your finances, first thank God for how your needs have been met in the past. If you are anxious about finding a mate, first thank God for the friends you have in your life. Whatever the case, start with praise and thanksgiving, and then present your request to God. Paul, without hesitation, stated that if we will habitually engage in this spiritual discipline as a primary means to ward off our anxiety, it will produce a certain outcome: "the peace of God, which transcends all understanding" (v. 7). Sign me up!

This is not just peace *from* God. That would be sufficient for me. But he is offering something more: the peace *of* God. He is making available to us the same level of tranquility that God himself has. That's next-level thinking. Paul said it "transcends all understanding." No kidding. This phrase translates to "that which rises above the mind." It is definitely beyond our pay grade. New Testament scholar Alfred Plummer wrote, "God's peace is able to produce exceedingly better results than human planning or that it is far superior to any person's schemes for security or that it is more effective for removing anxiety than any intellectual effort or power of reasoning."[7]

And it gets better. Paul said this peace will "guard your hearts and your minds in Christ Jesus" (v. 7). *Guard* is a military term that pictures a host of soldiers who stand guard over a city to protect it from attack. Philippi, as a Roman colony, had a Roman garrison around it to protect it. As soon as Paul mentioned this, the people would have gotten a strong image of what he was talking about. Yet, instead of the garrison being a bunch of human soldiers who can bleed and die, what is offered here is the impenetrable peace of God. Can someone shout out a hallelujah?

Paul finished by telling us that the peace of God sets up post around our hearts and minds. God protects our hearts from wrong feelings. God's peace protects our minds from wrong thinking. Most of our anxiety is based on lies. Once they get anchored internally, it is hard to get them to move out. This spiritual practice helps ensure wrong feelings and wrong thinking never break through and set up residence inside us.

For years, I used to feel guilty that I didn't pray that much. But I abandoned this emotion years ago. After wrestling with two long battles of clinical depression and anxiety in my life, I realized I am not courageous enough to live without prayer. I love the way C. S. Lewis put it: "I pray because I can't help myself. I pray because I'm helpless. I pray because the need flows out of me all the time, waking and sleeping. It doesn't change God. It changes me."[8]

Paul invited you to join the band, to experience a peace that exists even when the circumstances cannot be changed. What is not to love about this?

## HOW APPRECIATION CUTS OFF ANXIETY

I've said it before, but oftentimes I feel that if I worry about something hard enough, maybe it won't happen. Of course, that is untrue, but I can't seem to help myself sometimes, even when I'm regularly coming to the Lord in prayer. Does that ever happen to you?

The problem with our prayers is that we focus them on our problems. This is the power of Paul's slight tweak to our prayer time. Adding thanksgiving in front of and during our requests changes everything.

The practice of thanksgiving is all about appreciation. When we engage in the practice of appreciation, particularly through prayer, it creates what psychologists call a *perception shift*. Here is what happens in our brains during a prayer time that is sprinkled with appreciation:

The threatening messages from your amygdala and the anxious instincts of your brainstem are cut off, suddenly and surely, from access to your brain's neo-cortex, where they can fester, replicate themselves, and turn your stream of thoughts into a cold river of dread. It is a fact of neurology that the brain cannot be in a state of appreciation and a state of fear at the same time.[9]

An article on the "science of thought" had this to say: "If you change your attitude and determine to apply God's excellent advice not to worry, the hypothalamus will cause the secretion of chemicals that facilitate the feeling of peace."[10] Simply put, God gave us prayer to calm our nerves and help us overcome worry in a fallen world. It doesn't eliminate the object of our fear but reminds us that we have one on our side who is greater. God knew when he crafted Adam in the garden that his mind and body would respond to authentic, heartfelt, yet positive conversations with him. And it's the same for each one of us. I'm pretty sure Paul didn't know what we now know about the brain and how it functions. He merely wrote down what he was led to say through the inspiration of the Holy Spirit. Then he put it into practice and found that it worked. And the same will be true for us as we apply his teachings today. Eureka!

## GIVING YOUR WORRIES TO THE FATHER

Every summer as a boy, our family would travel a little over three hours by wood-paneled station wagon from Cleveland, Ohio, to southwest Pennsylvania to visit relatives. One summer day, two of my cousins and I took off on bicycles. We were heading to the top of the hill leading into the neighborhood. It was so steep that we had to walk our bikes up the last fifty yards or so. It was a dirt road, with the exception of that last fifty yards, which was heavily layered with gravel.

We got up to the top of the hill a little winded. But within seconds, we were back on our bikes with the wheels faced downhill. Away we went. Because of the incline, our speed increased quickly. The ride was bumpy due to the heavy gravel. Adrenaline was pumping throughout my body. I was living the dream!

Then, out of nowhere, the two handlebar grips on my bike came off and the front wheel immediately and suddenly turned perpendicular to the road. I went flying over the handlebars. While suspended in midair, I quickly made the decision to break my fall and protect my head (we didn't wear helmets back then) by sticking out my hands and arms to absorb the impact.

As my body made contact with the gravel, I could feel the skin breaking first on the palms of my hands, then my arms, and finally on my kneecaps. Turns out my cousins, as a joke, had poured dishwashing soap inside the handlebar grips so they would slide off. I stood up and immediately noticed the blood. Terror overcame me as I quickly scanned the extent of my injuries and began to process the betrayal of my cousins. As I took off in full stride, screaming, I kept shouting out only one word. Can you guess what that word was?

"Mom!"

I was screaming her name as I entered the house. She immediately jumped up and ran the rest of the way to me. As our eyes locked, with tears streaming down my face, I simply held out my arms. As soon as she touched my arm, my worry and anxiety washed away. I had officially given the problem to my mother, and she took it from there. I no longer needed to worry. She would know exactly what to do. It was her problem now, and she took on the assignment with great passion.

This is what Paul invited us to do. Instead of engaging in the unproductive and physically and psychologically damaging act of worrying, we should cry out, "Abba, Father" to our heavenly father (*Abba* is the Aramaic word for "daddy"). This is who Jesus cried out to when his anxiety overwhelmed him in the garden of Gethsemane on the night before his crucifixion (Mark 14:36). By the time he left the garden, his anxiety had subsided, and he was settled in his mind about what he needed to do, knowing his father was with him.

Paul recommended we do the same thing when we find ourselves overcome with anxiety:

> The Spirit you received does not make you slaves, so that you live in fear again; rather, the Spirit you received brought about your adoption to sonship. And by him we cry, *"Abba,* Father." (Romans 8:15)

So, the next time you find yourself flying over a set of handlebars headlong into worry, immediately get up and start running toward God to surrender what troubles you.

## THE JOY CHALLENGE

The challenge for this principle is obvious. We are going to practice what Paul advised. We are going to give what troubles us to God by presenting our requests to him with thanksgiving.

Start out by writing in your journal about your current requests. You may want to zero in on one issue, but try to keep the list to no more than three. Then, begin by praying Psalm 8. Read it to God as a personal letter from you. As you do, you will be reminded that God is bigger than your biggest fear. Let that soak in.

As you present your requests before God, identify something positive about this request. Then, in the words of Jesus, tell him what you want him to do for you. Be honest and very specific ("Rabbi, I want to see"). As you are praying, engage in a practice called "havening." This is a healing technique that helps boost serotonin production in the brain (which leads to satisfaction, happiness, optimism). This should physically help you calm down and feel a bit of release from the stress of the situation. Here are three different techniques for havening. Try all three, or focus on the one that really resonates with you.[11]

- Rub the palms of your hands together, slowly, as if you're washing your hands.
- Give yourself a hug. Place your hands on your opposite shoulders and rub them down your arms to your elbows.
- Place your fingertips up high on your forehead and then let your hands fall down your face to your chin.

Dr. Amen said, "From a neuroscience perspective, havening is a form of stimulating both sides of the brain (essential for healing) while you mentally bring up a stressful thought or past trauma."[12] By the way, the third technique works best for me.

When you are done, record your thoughts in your journal. If you found it helpful, consider making this a daily practice in your life.

> REMEMBER TO CARRY YOUR JOY CUBE WITH YOU EVERYWHERE YOU GO TODAY. MAKE SURE YOU POP IT OPEN SO YOU AND OTHERS CAN KEEP THE PRINCIPLES EVER BEFORE YOU. KEEP MEMORIZING PHILIPPIANS 4:6-7.

# REHEARSE YOUR BLESSINGS DAILY

*Finally, brothers and sisters, whatever is true, whatever is noble, whatever is right, whatever is pure, whatever is lovely, whatever is admirable—if anything is excellent or praiseworthy—think about such things. Whatever you have learned or received or heard from me, or seen in me—put it into practice. And the God of peace will be with you.*

–PHILIPPIANS 4:8-9

These two verses, coupled with the prior two, arguably make up the most potent advice for fighting off worry and anxiety in our lives. So, read on with great anticipation. Help is on the way!

Paul began with the word *finally*. It is by no means the end of the letter but merely the final imperative he offered to help us stand firm in this crazy world where it is superhard to have joy. Verses 8 and 9 are a single sentence in the Greek language. It forms yet another conditional clause: "*If* we do something first, *then* we can expect a certain outcome," which is peace (joy's cousin). The outcome is not automatic; we have a part to play. And we must go first.

In verse 8, Paul asked us to think a certain way. The action he asked us to take here is not just about comprehending a category of thought but habitually dwelling on it. It's a bit like marinating meat. When I prepare a steak (almost always a filet mignon), I marinate it in a special sauce for the entire day. Then I cook the steak to a temperature of about 120 degrees, before pulling it off the grill. As it sits on the serving tray, it continues to heat up to a perfect 125 degrees. No need for another sauce or ketchup to sit on top of the steak. Every single bite contains the amazing flavor it was bathed in. This is what Paul invited us to do here, to bathe our minds daily in our blessings.

The sauce I use has eight ingredients: soy, water, lime juice, vinegar, dried garlic, citric acid, paprika, and lime oil. The sauce Paul had in mind also has eight ingredients, or characteristics: true, noble, right, pure, lovely, admirable, excellent, and praiseworthy. He wanted our minds marinated in this life-giving sauce. If we do this, the outcome will be a soul-watering, worry-defying, worth-savoring peace. Let's take a closer look at these eight ingredients.

- **TRUE:** This can include things that are true and truthful in thought, word, or deed. Truth anchors our soul; it gives us a sense of stability and constancy. Research tells us that 92 percent of the things we worry about are imaginary and never come true. Satan is the father of lies (John 8:44), and he longs to corrupt our minds with things that just aren't true. That's why Paul warned the believers in Corinth, "But I am afraid that just as Eve was deceived by the serpent's cunning, your minds may somehow be led astray from your sincere and pure devotion to Christ" (2 Corinthians 11:3). Instead, let's marinate our minds in what is true.

- **NOBLE:** This includes things that are majestic, full of dignity, and awe-inspiring. Things like the coronation of a good king, or a father or mother who gets up in the wee hours of the morning to do a job he or she doesn't particularly love in order to provide for the family. Let's marinate our minds in what is noble.

- **RIGHT:** This is about what is just. It is giving God and people their due. It also celebrates when people satisfy their obligations. This can include giving God the glory for your success, saying sorry to someone you've intentionally or unintentionally hurt, or reading a historical account of an injustice being overturned. It's the right thing to do. Let's marinate our minds in what is right.

- **PURE:** This cuts to our motives and our actions. It also celebrates the beauty of innocence. It can include the divine artistry of a stream of clear water or the sacrificial love a mother has for her newborn child. The options are limitless. No time for the impure . . . too many real, unadulterated, authentic, and bright things to ponder. Let's marinate our minds in what is pure.

- **LOVELY:** This ingredient deals with anything that calls forth love. It is winsome and attractive. It refers to anything that exudes a welcoming fragrance that provides pleasure to all. This could be metaphoric or literal. It can include watching a couple who has been married for sixty years dance together or enjoying the pleasing perfume of a gardenia. Let's marinate our minds in what is lovely.

- **ADMIRABLE:** This trait exudes what is kind. It is action that wins people over. It purposefully avoids what is likely to give offense. It is someone that quietly lays down their rights for the sake of someone else. It is something that calls us to a higher plane of virtue. When we watch the care and sacrifice of a mother duck for her young, we cherish the moment. Or it can be as simple as the busy guy who patiently walks behind an elderly person with a cane in a crowded hallway. Let's marinate our minds in what is admirable.

- **EXCELLENT:** This refers to something that exceeds our expectations. It is something or someone that goes above and beyond. When I get the steak right, which is not all the time, my guests will say, "This is excellent!" That puts a smile on my face. It is reading about the new discoveries of how marvelously and intricately God has wired the human brain. For me, it can also be watching a professional golfer hit a shot to perfection. I involuntarily shake my head in amazement. What is it for you? Go ahead—think about it. Let's marinate our minds in what is excellent.

- **PRAISEWORTHY:** This is what we witness that merits our praise. It can be watching a sunrise or a sunset and being amazed by God. It can be witnessing a child with a learning disability overcome the odds and walk across the graduation stage. It is a couple who humbles themselves and digs deep to forgive each other and opt to keep their family together. Let's marinate our minds in what is praiseworthy.

Later on in our passage, in verse 9, Paul shifted his focus from having the right thinking to having the right practice. It is not enough to know about this formula for peace. You have to incorporate it into your everyday life. As a spiritual father and mentor, Paul offered up his personal practices as a model. He invited the Philippians to put into practice the things they have . . .

- **LEARNED FROM HIM:** We can't put into practice what we don't first know.
- **RECEIVED FROM HIM:** We have to decide whether we believe in it or not.
- **HEARD FROM HIM:** Paul diligently taught us the operating principles.
- **SEEN IN HIM:** Paul modeled these principles in his actual life in front of us.

Paul is our personal joy trainer. He is pulling out all the stops to motivate us, teach us, and model for us the lifestyle that leads to peace. Not just any old peace but the peace of God.

## THE POWER OF OUR THOUGHTS

Our thoughts are surprisingly powerful in how much they can affect our lives, whether negative or positive. They set our mindsets as we go about our days, and as we put those mindsets into practice, we discover the peace and joy we long for. What does that look like in practice? We can see Paul's formula for peace at work in a couple of different situations.

It is on display in one famous longitudinal study on happiness using the old diaries of Catholic nuns.[1] In this study, 180 nuns in their twenties from the School Sisters of Notre Dame were asked to journal their thoughts. After more than five decades had passed, researchers studied them to see what they could learn about the impact of positive emotional content. Here is what they discovered. The nuns who wrote more joyful content lived ten years longer on average than those nuns whose journal entries were negative or even just neutral. By age eighty-five, 90 percent of the happiest nuns were still alive, compared to only 34 percent of the least happy nuns.[2]

Paul was a man of deep faith who was inspired by God to write down these famous verses of Scripture to help increase our joy. Little did he know that well over nineteen hundred years later, science would validate his prescription of being intentional with where we direct our thoughts. God knew all along.

We can also see this principle work itself out in the life of Darryl Burton. In 1984, a drug dealer was shot and killed at a gas station in St. Louis, Missouri. Although a witness described the murderer as a five-foot, six-inch-tall, light-skinned African American male, the authorities pinned the crime on a five-foot, ten-inch-tall, dark-skinned African American man named Darryl Burton. Two men came forward and identified Darryl as the murderer. It was later discovered that these men were awaiting trial and were offered a lighter sentence if they testified that Darryl was guilty. To add insult to injury, the public defender assigned to Darryl spent only one hour with him before the trial. And then, in less than one hour, the jury found him guilty. At the age of twenty-two, he was sentenced to life in prison.

Darryl clearly remembers a huge banner that hung at the entrance of the penitentiary that said, "Welcome to the Missouri State Pen. Leave all your hopes, family, and dreams behind." He recalled, "When I saw that banner, it deeply affected me and I lost all hope. I hated the place, the system, and anyone that had anything to do with it. It was hell on earth—filled with violence, evil, and hate."[3] How do you maintain your sanity when you are serving a life sentence for something you didn't do?

At first, not so well, I learned. In a personal conversation I had with Darryl, he told me he spent most of his time ruminating on all the lies that were told about him. He focused on the injustice that was delivered to him in a country where this isn't supposed to happen. He kept applying for a new trial, but time and time again he was rejected. His mind dwelt heavily on these rejections. The outcome was not peace but quite the opposite: hate, rage, and unforgiveness. Anger had a fierce grip on him. This was Darryl's life for the sixteen years between 1984 and 2000.

In 1998, as a nonbeliever, he wrote Jesus a letter: "Jesus, if you're real and help me get out of this place, not only will I serve you, but I'll tell the world about you." Well, two years later, that prayer started to be answered, and it changed everything for Darryl.

For ten years, Darryl had been part of a group called Centurion, an organization that works with incarcerated men and women who are innocent. They told him they believed in his innocence but that it would take ten years for them to get around to his case. Ten years later, in the year 2000, they were finally able to turn their focus to Darryl.

It was at this time that Darryl trusted Jesus as his Savior and Lord. His mind shifted from all the negativity he'd been dwelling on to Scripture. He immediately connected the dots between himself and Jesus. Jesus was also an innocent man who was condemned to die. Jesus even had eight different people declare his innocence, and yet the authorities still executed him. Right before Jesus breathed his last breath, he prayed, "Father, forgive them, for they do not know what they are doing" (Luke 23:34). The lights come on in Darryl's mind. He had tried and tried to forgive the people who had done this to him, but he couldn't. Then he realized that Jesus didn't forgive the people who were unjust to him. Rather, he asked the Father to forgive them through Jesus. This became Darryl's daily meditation and prayer.

As he marinated his mind in scriptures, he learned that Jesus invites us to love our enemies and pray for them. His mind was shifting from hate to love. New branches began to grow in his brain with a new kind of fruit budding at the end: love, joy, peace, patience, forbearance, kindness, goodness, faithfulness, gentleness, and self-control (Galatians 5:22–23). Darryl's mind was now focused on what was true, noble, right, pure, lovely, admirable, excellent, and praiseworthy.

One of the guards even said to him, "Hey, man, you are walking around here like you are free." Darryl replied, "I'm free. Whether or not they ever let me out of here, I am free." He was experiencing the peace of God despite the fact he was in prison for something he didn't do. Darryl said to me, "God had to work something out of me (bitterness and hatred) in order to work something into me (love and grace), in order to do his work through me."

It would take eight more years before Darryl was exonerated and released from prison. He spent just under twenty-five years of his life locked away for something he didn't do. After he was released, Darryl went to school and got a degree in theology. He now serves as one of the pastors of the largest Methodist church in America that just happens to be in the same town where I serve (that's how we know each other). And he also leads an organization called the Miracle of Innocence that seeks to advocate for Innocent people in prison.[4] To date, they have seen four innocent people, just like Darryl, freed. Darryl not only thinks about such things as truth and justice, but he practices them—and the God of peace is with him.

## THE JOY CHALLENGE

When I was a kid, we used to play the game "I Spy," particularly to make the time pass on long road trips. You select who is going to be the first spy. Then the spy identifies an object. Making sure you are not looking directly at the object, you say, "I spy something . . ." and then you give its color. The other people start guessing. Whoever guesses the object first gets to be the next spy. To mix things up, you can identify the object's shape or the first letter of the object's name. We had a blast playing this game growing up.

For our Joy Challenge, I want you to play the "I Spy" game, but you don't need any other players besides yourself and God. Throughout the day, I want you to look for situations or people that display the eight ingredients that lead to peace, ones that are true, noble, right, pure, lovely, admirable, excellent, and praiseworthy. When you spy it, describe it in your journal. Write it down in the form of a short prayer to God. Your goal is to find at least one thing for all eight categories. Feel free to invite some other folks to help you spy. Good luck.

REMEMBER TO CARRY YOUR JOY CUBE WITH YOU EVERYWHERE YOU GO TODAY. MAKE SURE YOU POP IT OPEN SO YOU AND OTHERS CAN KEEP THE PRINCIPLES EVER BEFORE YOU. KEEP MEMORIZING PHILIPPIANS 4:6-7.

# ACCEPT THAT MORE MONEY AND STUFF ISN'T THE ANSWER

*I rejoiced greatly in the Lord that at last you renewed your concern for me. Indeed, you were concerned, but you had no opportunity to show it. I am not saying this because I am in need, for I have learned to be content whatever the circumstances. I know what it is to be in need, and I know what it is to have plenty. I have learned the secret of being content in any and every situation, whether well fed or hungry, whether living in plenty or in want. I can do all this through him who gives me strength.*

—PHILIPPIANS 4:10-13

Abraham Lincoln was walking down the street with his two sons, who were crying and fighting. "What's the matter with the boys?" a friend asked. "The same thing that's wrong with the whole world," Lincoln replied. "I have three walnuts and each of the boys wants two!"[1]

In our next passage, Paul addressed the thing that most of us, at least at some time in our life, thought was the secret to joy—namely, more money and more stuff. But Paul said just the opposite. That's why our next joy principle is about accepting that more stuff and money isn't the answer. Let's unpack his thinking.

In verse 10, Paul used the word we have come to expect in this letter: *rejoice*. Paul was over the moon with joy that the Philippian believers were concerned about him. But he quickly wanted them to know that his joy was not dependent upon their gift. His increased joy came because of their love and sacrifice for him. His joy was not beholden to his circumstances.

Paul possessed a superpower, and it was something that he learned over time. What was the superpower? Contentment regardless of the circumstances. New Testament scholar M. R. Vincent explained that this describes the person who, through discipline, has become independent of external circumstances and has discovered within himself resources that are more than adequate for any situation that might arise.[2] Paul was declaring that he had acquired the virtue of a spirit free from worry of the vicissitudes of external events, both people and things.

If we are to ever get off the merry-go-round of mood swings, we, too, must learn this virtue. He then explained what he meant. Pay careful attention. Twice in verse 12 he stated, "I know." What he was really saying was more than just attaining book knowledge or comprehending a concept. He learned a skill, the skill of how to cope in the full spectrum of circumstances.

First, he informed us he learned to be content when he was in need. The word *need* draws up the image of something being lowered. It denotes a going down into deprivation, whether self-imposed or imposed by external forces. Paul said, "I have been here many times, and my joy count is no longer affected one iota by it." This is a game changer.

Paul then threw in the unexpected. He informed us that he also learned how to be content when he was living in plenty. If you are like me, you are thinking, *I don't need to learn how to be content when I have more than enough.* Oh yes, we do.

Some of the most miserable people in our world are those who live in extreme abundance. In fact, their resources have given them more weapons with which to destroy their lives and the lives of the people around them. Paul used the phrase "well fed" (v. 12) to describe this life. This phrase referred to animals that were force-fed to fatten them up for the slaughter. When it is all said and done, prosperity does more damage to followers of Jesus than adversity. Paul learned how not to fall for this. In the same way privations could do him no harm, so he was equally immune from harm when fortune smiled.[3]

Paul then informed us that he had learned the secret. It wasn't automatic. He had to learn this through the many seasons of ups and downs. He was now finally initiated into the secrets and privileges of this way of life that rises above the pitfalls of both poverty and prosperity. The secret to the superpower is now revealed: "I can do all this through him who gives me strength" (v. 13).

Paul was clearly referring to Christ. Remember in 3:7–10, how Paul was striving to know the power of Jesus' resurrection? Christ's resurrection was empowered by the Holy Spirit, who now lives in us (Romans 6:10–11; 8:11; Ephesians 1:19–20; 1 Peter 3:18). When we learn how to yield to the will of God, it activates the power of God within us to overcome the highs and lows of life that seek to drive us to anxiety and depression.[4]

The writer of Hebrews reinforced the message of this secret spiritual sauce: "Keep your lives free from the love of money and be content with what you have, because God has said, 'Never will I leave you; never will I forsake you'" (13:5). Being emancipated from the love of money, which can buy us stuff we soon lose interest in and gives us a false sense of security, is key for people who have it and for those who want it. The secret of our independence is our dependence on God, pure and simple.

God's joy is not dependent on money or stuff. Contentment is possible with it or without it. This means that if you have stuff, it is not a bad thing, as long as you don't depend on it as your source of joy. This is particularly hard for people who live in relatively economically flourishing areas like the United States. Someone once noted, "Americans define success as the next purchase, while other places in the world define success as a meal with family and friends." We chase hard after a purchase we truly believe will make us happy. But soon after we get it, the shine wears off and all we are left with are the monthly payments. So, what do we do? We learn our lesson and stop this cyclical nonsense that psychologists call the *hedonic treadmill*, which gets us nowhere, right? Unfortunately, we often just keep setting our sights on another shiny object.

Paul said there is nothing wrong with stuff. He had numerous seasons of plenty. We just need to be careful. We get into trouble when we expect our money and stuff to do for us what it was never intended to do.

In Paul's letter to his prodigy, Timothy, he instructed him to school the wealthy with this teaching: "Command those who are rich in this present world not to be arrogant nor to put their hope in wealth, which is so uncertain, but to put their hope in God, who richly provides us with everything for our enjoyment" (1 Timothy 6:17). God gives us everything for our enjoyment. When we put our hope in these things versus in God, we always end up empty. In a nutshell, whether you have three walnuts or no walnuts, you're good.

## CONTENTMENT REGARDLESS OF STUFF

In the 1500s, Nicolaus Copernicus discovered that the earth orbits around the sun, not the other way around. Much like that paradigm-smashing discovery, recent advances in psychology and neuroscience have taught us that success revolves around happiness, not the other way around.[5]

Consider the work of Dr. Ronnie Janoff-Bulman on the contentment level of lottery winners.[6] He compared twenty-two winners of major lotteries with twenty-two average people and twenty-nine victims of paralysis. The lottery winners did report a temporary rush of merriment, but ultimately they were no happier than the average people in the study. As a matter of fact, they had lost the ability to find joy in the small pleasures of life.

Here is the shocker. Once the folks with paralysis got over the initial shock of their misfortune, they were not nearly as unhappy as you might expect. They also had a greater capacity to enjoy the smaller pleasures in life as compared to the lottery winners. The people dealing with a life of paralysis were more optimistic about future happiness than the lottery winners.

The problem is that no one feels they have enough. In a recent Gallup poll, the respondents believed that 21 percent of Americans were rich. Yet, only half of 1 percent believed they themselves were rich. So, we all keep chasing a goal that's always just beyond our reach. Consider this story.

An American investment banker was at the pier of a small coastal Mexican village when a small boat with just one local fisherman docked. Inside the small boat were several large yellowfin tunas. The American complimented the fisherman on the quality of his fish and asked how long it took to catch them.

The fisherman replied, "Only a little while."

The American then asked why he didn't stay out longer and catch more fish.

The fisherman said he had enough to support his family's immediate needs.

The American then asked, "But what do you do with the rest of your time?"

The fisherman said, "I sleep late, fish a little, play with my children, take siestas with my wife, Maria, stroll into the village each evening where I sip wine, and play guitar with my amigos. I have a full and busy life."

The American scoffed. "I have a Harvard MBA and could help you. You should spend more time fishing and, with the proceeds, buy a bigger boat. With the proceeds from the bigger boat, you could buy several boats. Eventually you would have a fleet of fishing boats. Instead of selling your catch to a middleman, you would sell directly to the processor, eventually opening your own cannery. You would control the product, processing, and distribution. You would need to leave this small coastal fishing village and move to Mexico City, then LA, and eventually New York City, where you would run your expanding enterprise."

The fisherman asked, "But how long will this all take?"

The American replied, "Fifteen to twenty years."

"But what then?" asked the fisherman.

The American laughed and said, "That's the best part. When the time is right, you would announce going public with an IPO and sell your company stock to the public and become very rich. You would make millions!"

"Millions? Then what?"

The American said, "Then you would retire, move to a small coastal fishing village where you would sleep late, fish a little, play with your kids, take siestas with your wife, stroll to the village in the evenings where you could sip wine and play your guitar with your amigos."

For many of us, we've convinced ourselves we need to work hard so that one day we can enjoy the fruit of our labor, when it has been sitting in front of us all along. Enjoying the things God provides doesn't require a ton of money and possessions. Paul said that God would supply all our needs but not necessarily all our wants. I think for many of us, we are not stressing out and working hard to meet our needs but to support our chosen lifestyle because we believe it will make us happier. There is absolutely no evidence that this will be the case.

When money and stuff become too important to our happiness and well-being, it creates all kinds of stress in our lives. A Harvard study showed that men who experience elevated chronic anxiety are six times more likely than contented men to die from a sudden heart attack.[7] Our pursuit for more stuff is killing us. We must learn the secret of contentment regardless of our stuff.

## THE JOY CHALLENGE

I am going to give you two options for your challenge this time.

One option is to give away something you own that you really like to someone who would enjoy it or could even use it more than you do. This will help you get a read on where you are with putting your joy in your stuff. Journal your thoughts after the transaction is complete.

The other option is to lean into the wealth that is more than just stuff or money. After dinner, if the weather permits, pull some comfy chairs onto the front porch or driveway. Invite a few friends or neighbors over, and spend the evening with them. Bring out your beverage of choice and have extra available for whoever else stops by. If it is a bit chilly and you have a portable firepit, fire it up, or bring out some blankets for people to wrap up in. Consider putting on some music, but not too loud so people can talk. Share your favorite childhood stories, or just stare up into the sky and listen to the music. If possible, have these people over for dinner beforehand. Keep it super simple. Throw some burgers or brats on the grill, order your favorite pizza, or have everyone bring a dish.

After everyone goes home, journal your thoughts on this experience. Remember the quote from earlier: "In America we define success as the next purchase; in other parts of the world, they define success as an evening meal with family and friends."

REMEMBER TO CARRY YOUR JOY CUBE WITH YOU EVERYWHERE YOU GO TODAY. MAKE SURE YOU POP IT OPEN SO YOU AND OTHERS CAN KEEP THE PRINCIPLES EVER BEFORE YOU. KEEP MEMORIZING PHILIPPIANS 4:6-7.

# LET PEOPLE HELP YOU

*Yet it was good of you to share in my troubles. Moreover, as you Philippians know, in the early days of your acquaintance with the gospel, when I set out from Macedonia, not one church shared with me in the matter of giving and receiving, except you only; for even when I was in Thessalonica, you sent me aid more than once when I was in need. Not that I desire your gifts; what I desire is that more be credited to your account. I have received full payment and have more than enough. I am amply supplied, now that I have received from Epaphroditus the gifts you sent. They are a fragrant offering, an acceptable sacrifice, pleasing to God. And my God will meet all your needs according to the riches of his glory in Christ Jesus.*

**—PHILIPPIANS 4:14–19**

As we come to the end of this amazing letter, Paul finished by thanking the Philippians for the gift they sent through Epaphroditus. It is proper to acknowledge when people give you a gift. But there is so much more going on here. He already told them at the opening of the letter that their partnership in supporting him brought him joy (1:4). In 4:10, he wrote, "I rejoiced greatly in the Lord that at last you renewed your concern for me." He communicated the same thing to the believers in Corinth: "He [Titus] told us about your longing for me, your deep sorrow, your ardent concern for me, so that my joy was greater than ever" (2 Corinthians 7:7).

When other people help us at our point of need, it increases our joy. When a need we have is selflessly supplied by others with no ulterior motive, it lifts our burden and frees us of worry and anxiety. This is pretty universal and straightforward. Yet, as you read this paragraph and peer between the lines and observe the language Paul used, you might feel that he was not quite comfortable with the whole thing. Maybe he was experiencing what Jesus taught us: "It is more blessed to give than to receive" (Acts 20:35). Remember, the word *blessed* simply means "happy." Giving makes one happier than receiving.

Paul expressed his struggle with this to the believers in Thessalonica: "Surely you remember, brothers and sisters, our toil and hardship; we worked night and day in order not to be a burden to anyone while we preached the gospel of God to you" (1 Thessalonians 2:9). Then, in his second letter to them, he wrote, "Nor did we eat anyone's food without paying for it. On the contrary, we worked night and day, laboring and toiling so that we would not be a burden to any of you" (2 Thessalonians 3:8).

Paul didn't want to be a burden to anyone. I think many of us feel this way. We are extremely busy people and know how hard it is to fit everything into a given day. So, when we are down on our luck, we feel bad that people who are as busy as we are or as strapped as we are financially would sacrifice for us. The gift of precious time or money humbles us.

Paul also didn't want anyone to think he was in it for the money. Even though he clearly taught that teachers and leaders in the church deserve a wage for their labor (1 Timothy 5:17), he still struggled to think that people might question his motives and somehow reject Christ. So, in addition to his already rigorous schedule, he added tent-making to his daily grind (Acts 18:3). I am assuming that Paul could continue to make tents and sell them for the two years he was under house arrest, but I am not completely sure about that. If not, this would have put him in a very difficult place resource-wise. Paul was bold when he asked for money for others (2 Corinthians 8–9), but he struggled to receive it from others for himself. I think most of us are the same way.

In verse 14, Paul wrote, "It was good of you to share in my troubles." The word *good* in the Greek can translate to "beautifully good." Ralph Martin quipped, "Thus in this idiomatic expression, Paul comes as close to saying 'Thank you' as ever he does in this letter."[1] Paul then tempered his thanks by employing so many sterile banking terms when he referred to the assistance that they gave him. In verse 15, he used the phrase "giving and receiving," which, in the ancient world of commerce, referred to the debit and credit sides of the ledger. Then, in verse 17, he declared that the central issue was not his desire for the gift but the credit to their account, which, once again, used a banking term to cast the Philippians' gift as a spiritual investment, which would increasingly pay them rich dividends from God.[2] In verse 18, he informed them he had received "full payment." This is like giving them a tax-deductible receipt for their gift. He then announced that he was "amply supplied." This is another way of saying, "I am not expecting you to send me anything more."

But as the letter comes to a close, Paul shifted from the language of banking to the language of worship. He proclaimed that the ultimate recipient of the gift is not him but God. This is no doubt taken out of the teaching of Jesus. Jesus taught us that whenever we . . .

- give food to the hungry,
- offer drink to the thirsty,
- invite a stranger into our home,
- give clothes to the naked, or
- visit those in prison.

. . . it is as though we do it directly to Jesus. Jesus said, "Truly I tell you, whatever you did for one of the least of these brothers and sisters of mine, you did for me" (Matthew 25:40). The Philippians meant for Paul to be the gainer from their generosity, and so indeed he was, but on the spiritual plane, the permanent gain was theirs.[3]

Paul wrapped up his comments by stating a promise to those who are generous: "And my God will meet all your needs according to the riches of his glory in Christ Jesus" (v. 19). I love the way Paul referred to God as "my God." Paul had a long history of experiencing the power and provision of God to meet all his personal needs. His relationship with God was up close and personal.

Hudson Taylor, the legendary missionary to China, wrote, "When God's work is done in God's way for God's glory, it will not lack for God's supply."[4] We give out of our poverty, but God supplies our needs on a scale worthy of his worth.

At the end of each day, I believe Paul laid his head on his crummy prison-provided pillow and wept as he pondered the years the Philippian believers had come to his aid. They made his burden lighter. They were never asked to help; they wanted to out of their love and respect for Paul. Without question, this decreased Paul's worry and increased his joy. Even though we don't want to, we need to be open to our last joy principle, which is letting people help us.

As we have seen, it not only increases the joy of the recipient; it ultimately increases the joy of the giver even more.

## THE JOY OF GIVING AND RECEIVING

There has been a ton of research on the positive outcomes of giving to and serving others.

According to a study in *Social Science & Medicine*, a person who volunteers more than monthly but less than weekly is 12 percent more likely to report being very happy, and a person who volunteers weekly is 16 percent more likely to report being very happy.[5] Giving support to others may also have greater benefits for the one giving than the person receiving help, thus reinforcing the teaching of Jesus.

How does giving and serving others impact our brains?

Emiliana Simon-Thomas, the science director at the Greater Good Science Center at UC Berkeley, has led some helpful studies in this area. The research shows that spending money on someone other than yourself promotes happiness. Why? Giving a loved one something they truly want or donating to a charity that means something to you "creates more interaction between the parts of the brain associated with processing social information and feeling pleasure."[6] People call this phenomenon the "warm glow," the intrinsic delight in doing something for someone else.

Dr. Simon-Thomas explained that when we give to and serve others, it not only releases dopamine (the pleasure hormone) in our brains but also "activates pathways in the brain that release oxytocin, which is a neuropeptide [protein-like molecules] that signals trust, safety, and connection. It's often referred to as the 'cuddle hormone.'"[7]

Decades of research have also shown that gift giving and receiving can elicit similar brain responses: "If you're given a gift from someone who cares about you a lot and you really love what they have gotten you, that is going to yield a very similar oxytocin-laden reward response."[8] While it is more blessed to give than to receive, allowing someone else to help us, particularly when we are in a jam or have a need we can't seem to meet, gives us that sensation of God wrapping his loving arms around us (oxytocin release). It makes us feel we are not alone, that we are safe and that things are going to be alright. That just might increase one's joy level.

Letting others help you can also be the best gift you can give back to another person. What they do out of love to aid you will do more to bring that person joy than you. Don't rob that from them by refusing to receive their generosity laced in love.

## A BEAUTIFUL EXPERIENCE OF GRACE

Jennifer was a young woman who lived with her single-parent mom and her younger brother. They were getting by, but money was extremely tight. Jennifer had a vision to better her life by going to school to become a nurse. To save for her schooling, she worked several jobs. With each paycheck, she would set aside as much as she could in a small box she hid in her bedroom. Over the months, she was making small incremental progress toward her goal.

One evening, she came home from work on a Saturday night and opened the box, only to find that the money was all gone except for ten dollars. She immediately knew what had happened. Her younger brother had stolen it to use for drugs. She was devastated and defeated.

The next morning, she drove to the church where I was the pastor. She was so angry at her brother, she almost didn't come in, but at the last minute before the service was to start, she pulled herself together and came inside. That morning, I was speaking on generosity. At the end of the message, Jennifer did two very courageous things. One, she forgave her brother. Two, she took the remaining ten dollars and placed it in the offering plate.

She wrote me a handwritten note to share her story and to tell me what she had done as a result of my message. It was meant to encourage me. She placed the letter in a blank envelope with no signature or return address and dropped it off at the church the next day. I was moved by the letter and her display of spiritual obedience but had no way of contacting her. I decided to use her story in my next Sunday's message. I knew it would inspire so many people.

At the end of the first of three services, two couples came down to the front of the church with tears in their eyes and shared that they were moved to pay for Jennifer's nursing schooling—100 percent of it. In the next service, I read the letter and made this announcement: "If the person who wrote this letter is in the service, please come see me." Jennifer just happened to be in that service, and she came down and introduced herself to me. I got to tell her about what the two families wanted to do, and she began to weep.

If you have ever been in this spot, you know it is a humbling place to be. As Jesus said, "It is more blessed to give than to receive." At the end of the day, she decided to let these good people help her. Four years later Jennifer finished nursing school at the top of her class and debt-free. Today, she is married with two children and is an oncology nurse. She is living out the mission God has given her. Last time we talked, her heart was filled with joy.

I have also talked to the two families who met Jennifer's need. To this day, they consider it to be one of the biggest joys of their lives. Because Jennifer let them help her, their joy was increased as well. Win-win! The cuddle hormone was swimming in the minds of a bunch of people through this beautiful experience of grace.

This is what Paul was trying to teach us. You want to increase your joy? Humble yourself, and let other people help you.

# THE JOY CHALLENGE

Many years ago, I had a neighbor named Tom who taught me an important principle I have never forgotten. The principle? Put yourself in a place of need. Let me give you an example.

One Saturday, early in our relationship, Tom came over to my house and asked if I had a ladder he could borrow. I did have a ladder and was delighted I could meet his need. Remember, this act of service and generosity released dopamine and oxytocin in my brain. I was feeling pretty good. Several weeks later, I was over at his house in his garage and noticed he had a ladder. I said, "Tom, I see you have a ladder. Why did you need to borrow mine?" He replied, "I never said I didn't have a ladder; I just asked if I could borrow yours."

I learned a very important lesson that day that I ultimately included in a book I wrote with my wife, Rozanne, called *Real Simplicity: Making Room for Life*. We often make friends by helping people. People feel better when they help us. Tom and I went on to become the best of friends.

How can you put yourself in a place of need today? That's your final Joy Challenge. Maybe there is a tool you need to purchase before you can work on that home project. Instead of buying the tool, try to find someone who already has it and humbly ask if you can borrow it. Maybe there is a decision you need to make, and you know someone who might have some expertise, knowledge, or a qualified opinion to offer. Reach out and ask. Another easy move is to ask your parents what they think, particularly if you are an adult child. Go to them. Put yourself in a place of need.

At the end of the day, take some time to journal your thoughts. How did this experience make you feel? How do you think the giver felt about the experience?

## LET PEOPLE HELP YOU

REMEMBER TO CARRY YOUR JOY CUBE WITH YOU EVERYWHERE YOU GO TODAY. MAKE SURE YOU POP IT OPEN SO YOU AND OTHERS CAN KEEP THE PRINCIPLES EVER BEFORE YOU. THIS WOULD BE A GOOD TIME TO REVIEW ALL FOUR OF THE PASSAGES YOU HAVE MEMORIZED OVER THE COURSE OF THIS CHALLENGE.

# CONCLUSION

# WRAPPING UP
# THE CHALLENGE

*To our God and Father be glory for ever and ever. Amen.*
*Greet all God's people in Christ Jesus. The brothers and*
*sisters who are with me send greetings. All God's people here*
*send you greetings, especially those who belong to Caesar's*
*household.*
*The grace of the Lord Jesus Christ be with your spirit.*
*Amen.*

**–PHILIPPIANS 4:20-23**

Paul concluded his beautiful letter by giving God all the glory.
Why, of course he did. This way of life—a joy despite our circumstances, other people, and our past, and a joy that defeats worry—is only possible because of God. So, we join in with Paul, with our hands lifted in the air, and give God glory for making this way of life available to us through Jesus Christ.

After a few greetings, Paul closed with a benediction: "The grace of the Lord Jesus Christ be with your spirit." Our spirit is that non-material part of us that is wrapped in human flesh. It is the part of us that lives on after our bodies give out. Some suggest that our spirit dwells in the upper part of our brain called the *ventrolateral frontal cortex*. This is the part of the brain that is completely unique to humans.[1] I think they may be onto something.

Paul didn't want our spirit, our brain, to be filled with laws and judgment. He wanted it to be filled with God's grace. God loves us; we don't have to earn it. God is for us, not against us. When we look at the face of God, we see the sparkle in his eyes that he is happy to be with us. Jesus longs for his joy to be complete in us. God is not out to get us; he is out to get us back into a relationship. He doesn't want us to live in fear; his perfect love casts out all our fears.

What did we do to deserve this? Not a single thing. That is why it is called grace. Stop asking questions and take it all in. That's what God wants you to do. That is why Jesus went to the cross, to fulfill the law and make grace available to us.

This twenty-five-day challenge has been designed to form the grace of God's joy as a habit in your life. The principles flowed directly out of the Bible's treatise on joy, the letter to the Philippians. Paul not only taught us these principles, but he modeled them for us as he sat under house arrest in Rome for two years. Paul uncovered the secret of joy despite all the things that came up against him to steal it away.

Over the last twenty-five days, you have been asked to . . .

- **READ:** Read the assigned chapter for the day.
- **DO:** Complete the Joy Challenge for each day.
- **MEMORIZE:** Memorize four key Scripture passages.
- **REVIEW:** Carry the Joy Cube with you everywhere.

In your first journal entry, found in chapter 1, you were asked to rate yourself in two categories: your current life circumstances, and the level of joy you were experiencing. Now it is time to revisit those questions in light of the twenty-five-day journey you have just completed.

1. Regarding the circumstances of your life:
   • Where were you twenty-five days ago? _____
   • Where are you today? _____
2. Regarding your current level of joy:
   • Where were you twenty-five days ago? _____
   • Where are you today? _____

Go back now and look at your answers. Your circumstances may not have changed. They may have gotten worse. I do hope, however, that your level of joy has gone up at least a little.

The last thing you need to do to complete the Joy Challenge is to invite someone new to the experience. If you want to take it over the top, consider gifting them the experience. You might even consider inviting a few more friends into the experience and forming a small group. Since you are familiar with the whole journey, you would be the perfect leader or, even better, a guide.

Once you finish this final step, you will have completed the Joy Challenge. Congratulations! What a journey it has been. And what gifts we have discovered along the way. We began this by praying for you. Let me finish it by praying for you again.

*Dear God,*

*Even though we have likely never met, I feel a special bond with the person reading this prayer. I prayed every day for them through this journey that they would at the very least get a taste of the joy you offer through Jesus. I pray earnestly that some of the storms of worry have settled down a bit in their life. More than that, I pray they feel more equipped to handle those storms and experience your joy despite them.*

*I pray the journey doesn't stop here until the brand of joy that Jesus offers is complete in them. Finally, I pray they feel your calling to spread this joy with everyone they encounter until they see you face-to-face. Maybe in your new kingdom granted to us through faith in your Son, we can finally meet and share our journeys in your joy.*

*The grace of the Lord Jesus Christ be with their spirit. Amen.*

# ACKNOWLEDGMENTS

Paul opened the book of Philippians with a word of thanksgiving: "I thank my God every time I remember you" (v. 3). As I recall the people who have been a part of my journey to bring this book to fruition, I feel the same way as Paul when he wrote a few verses later, "It is right for me to feel this way about all of you, since I have you in my heart" (v. 7). The Philippians brought Paul joy. The people I acknowledge below bring me joy.

I dedicate this book to the congregation I serve at Westside Family Church. Over the years I have had the privilege to serve as your pastor, you have refreshed me and restored me in the most amazing and gracious ways. You don't give yourselves over to pettiness and squabbles but lean into your faith with great gusto. It has been my honor to serve you as an under-shepherd of Jesus. You bring me joy.

I must mention specifically the elders I serve alongside at Westside: Dan Chaverin, Jeff Manford, Brad Norman, Matt Adams, Troy Kennedy, JJ Lane, Kenny Conklin, and Rick Perkins. It is amazing what can be accomplished when we truly align our lives to the values of love, integrity, Spirit-led decision-making, empowerment, and gracious excellence. It's all about Jesus, right? You bring me joy.

# ACKNOWLEDGMENTS

My assistant, Laura Saville, continues to do heroic feats to hold my life and ministry together. I take on more than I should, but Laura helps make it all come together. And Lyssa Kirwan and her team have been a huge support not only in my work at Westside but around the globe. You bring me joy.

I was reflecting the other day on the number of older men who, for whatever reason, chose to come alongside me to mentor and support me. Many of them have gone on to be with God, and it has left a hole in my heart: Bob Buford, Dallas Willard, George Gallup Jr., Howard Hendricks, and Lyle Schaller. I am grateful to still have you, Mike Reilly and Ron Doornink, in my life. You have offered unconditional support and encouragement to me that puts fuel in my tank and enables me to soar. You bring me joy.

Neighbors have always been a very important part of our lives. It is the royal command of Scripture. Proximity promotes depth of relationship. We are truly there for one another. Once a neighbor with the Frazees, always a neighbor. I call out my neighbors of Cottonwood Canyon and my neighbors in Cordillera Ranch. Doing life with you is a rush. You bring me joy.

I have been blessed with an amazing family. Our four children have not only been a driving inspiration for all I do but they have also become great friends and supporters, along with their partners. Thank you, Jennifer and Desmond, David and Gretchen, Stephen and Fonda, and Austin and Kelly. You bring me joy. I must also make mention of my sister, Teresa, and her husband, Gary. My sister knows her poor brother needs extra love and help, and she and Gary provide it with intentionality and grace. You bring me joy.

I single out my five grandchildren and the ones yet to come. If you are a grandparent, you get it. Ava, Crew, Gabriela, Yoana, and Aneliya, you occupy my mind in many of the moments of my waking hours. I am rooting for you in the most intense way. I am so proud of you. You bring me joy.

There is deep gratitude in my heart for my partnership with HarperCollins Christian Publishing, under the leadership of my long-time friend Mark Schoenwald. We have journeyed arm in arm since 2000. This last quarter of a century has been awesome. My editor, Jessica Rogers, is amazing. Gracious excellence defines her work style. I couldn't have done it without you. Beth Murphy from Church Source has been like a sister to me over all these years. I would take a bullet for you. John Raymond and I met years ago at a young leaders conference. It has been a minute since then. I love all that we have done and have yet to do together. You bring me joy.

You cannot publish without a good agent, and I have the best. Don Gates is not only supersmart and dedicated to his work, but he is my advocate and friend. Let's keep dreaming together, brother. You bring me joy.

In every book I have written, I mention Ray and Mary Graham. They were my neighbors when I was just a boy living in Cleveland, Ohio. They were the ones who reached out to me and invited me to their church. It was through them I became a follower of Jesus. My relationship with Christ means everything to me. He has given me meaning and purpose and eternal life. Amazing grace, how sweet the sound. How could I ever forget the ones who introduced him to me? Ray and Mary, you bring me joy.

Finally, I thank the "wife of my youth," as Solomon called her. I started sitting next to Rozanne in church when I was fifteen years old. We got married when I was twenty. We have grown up together and have experienced the most amazing life together. Rozanne believes in me and still laughs at my jokes. We spend virtually every moment of every day together. That's the way I like it. She also helps me edit my books before they go to the publisher. (Jessica, the manuscript was in worse shape before Rozanne got a hold of it.) Rozanne, if you will keep having me, I will be with you to the very end. You bring me joy!

# NOTES

## INTRODUCTION

1. "Declaration of Independence: A Transcription," U.S. National Archives and Records Administration, last reviewed October 11, 2023, https://www.archives.gov/founding-docs/declaration-transcript.

2. John F. Helliwell et al., "World Happiness Report 2022," *World Happiness Report*, March 8, 2022, https://worldhappiness.report/ed /2022/happiness-benevolence-and-trust-during-covid-19-and-beyond /#ranking-of-happiness-2019-2021.

3. Jukka Savolainen, "The Grim Secret of Nordic Happiness," Slate, April 28, 2021, https://slate.com/news-and-politics/2021/04/finland -happiness-lagom-hygge.html.

4. Savolainen, "The Grim Secret."

5. Stephen Trotter, "Breaking the Law of Jante," *eSharp* Issue 23, April 15, 2015, University of Glasgow, https://www.gla.ac.uk/media /Media_404385_smxx.pdf.

6. Finlo Rohrer, "The Apprentice: A Lesson from Sweden," May 7, 2013, *BBC Magazine*, https://www.bbc.com/news/magazine-22398633.

7. Warren W. Wiersbe, *Be Joyful: Even When Things Go Wrong, You Can Have Joy* (Wheaton: Victor Books, 1989), 15.

8. Jason Wachob, "Yes, You Can Change Your Brain: How to Do It in 5 Steps, From a Neuroscientist," MBG Health, July 15, 2020, https://

www.mindbodygreen.com/articles/5-steps-to-change-your-brain-from
-neuroscientist.

## PART 1: JOY DESPITE YOUR CIRCUMSTANCES

1. Lawrence O. Richards, *Expository Dictionary of Bible Words* (Grand Rapids: Zondervan, 1985), 361.
2. Gerald F. Hawthorne, Ralph P. Martin, and Daniel G. Reid, *The Dictionary of Paul and His Letters* (Westmont, IL: IVP Academics, 1993), 713.
3. Charles R. Swindoll, *Life Is 10% What Happens to You and 90% How You React* (Nashville: Thomas Nelson, 2023).
4. Viktor E. Frankl, *Man's Search for Meaning* (Boston: Beacon Press, 2014), 62.
5. Jennifer Rothschild, Living Beyond Limits, https://www.jenniferrothschild.com/about/.

## PRINCIPLE #1: RECALL HAPPY MEMORIES

1. The first gift came when he was in Thessalonica (Philippians 4:16); the second gift came while he was in Corinth (2 Corinthians 11:9); and the third gift was the one he was now receiving while in Rome.
2. Gerald F. Hawthorne, *Philippians*, *Word Biblical Commentary*, vol. 43 (Waco, TX: Word Books, 1983), 24.
3. John F. Walvoord, *Philippians: Triumph in Christ* (Chicago: Moody Press, 1971), 29.
4. Jim Wilder and Michael Hendricks, *The Other Half of Church: Christian Community, Brain Science, and Overcoming Spiritual Stagnation* (Chicago: Moody Publishers, 2020), 52.
5. Christine Koh, "It's Time to Become Friends with Your Anxiety," CNN, updated October 6, 2021, https://www.cnn.com/2021/10/06/health/anxiety-wendy-suzuki-wellness/index.html.
6. "Meditation: A Simple, Fast Way to Reduce Stress," Mayo Clinic, April 29, 2022, https://www.mayoclinic.org/tests-procedures/meditation/in-depth/meditation/art-20045858.
7. Wilder and Hendricks, *The Other Half of Church*, 52.
8. Adapted from Martin E. P. Seligman, *Flourish* (New York: Free Press, 2011), chapter 2.

## PRINCIPLE #2: LEARN HOW TO LOVE

1. Gerald F. Hawthorne, *Philippians, Word Biblical Commentary*, vol. 43 (Waco: Word Books, 1983), 26.

2. John F. Walvoord, *Philippians: Triumph in Christ* (Chicago: Moody Press, 1971), 30.

3. "Sine Cera," *The Guardian*, October 19, 2004, https://www.theguardian.com/books/2004/oct/19/poetry12.

4. *Agape* is used in the New Testament to refer to an unconditional and sacrificial love for others. It is a love that originates with God, who is Love.

5. Gerald F. Hawthorne, Ralph R. Martin, and Daniel G. Reid, *The Dictionary of Paul and His Letters* (Westmont, IL: IVP Academics, 1993), 512.

6. Robert Waldinger, MD, and Marc Schulz, PhD, *The Good Life: Lessons from the World's Longest Scientific Study of Happiness* (New York: Simon and Schuster, 2023).

7. Robert Waldinger and Marc Schulz, "The Lifelong Power of Close Relationships," *Wall Street Journal*, January 13, 2023, https://www.wsj.com/articles/the-lifelong-power-of-close-relationships-11673625450.

8. "Loneliness Twice As Unhealthy As Obesity for Older People, Study Finds," *The Guardian*, February 16, 2014, https://www.theguardian.com/science/2014/feb/16/loneliness-twice-as-unhealthy-as-obesity-older-people and https://www.ncbi.nlm.nih.gov/pmc/articles/PMC7437541/.

9. Gary Chapman, *The Five Love Languages:The Secret to Love that Lasts* (1992; repr. New York: Northfield Publishing, 2015).

## PRINCIPLE #3: SEE THE GLASS AS HALF-FULL

1. Warren W. Wiersbe, *Be Joyful: Even When Things Go Wrong, You Can Have Joy* (Wheaton, IL: Victor Books, 1989), 38.

2. F. F. Bruce, *Philippians: New International Biblical Commentary* (Peabody, MA: Hendrickson Publishers, 1989), 41.

3. Acts 24:24–27; 25:1–26.

4. Wiersbe, *Be Joyful*, 39.

5. Wiersbe, *Be Joyful*.

6. F. F. Bruce, *Philippians*, 47–48.

7. Shawn Achor, "The Happy Secret to Better Work," filmed May 2011 in Bloomington, Indiana, Ted video, 12:17, https://www.ted.com/talks/shawn_achor_the_happy_secret_to_better_work?language=en.

8. Daniel Amen, *You, Happier: The 7 Neuroscience Secrets of Feeling Good Based on Your Brain Type* (Carol Stream, IL: Tyndale, 2022), 128.

9. Caroline Leaf, *Switch On Your Brain: The Key to Peak Happiness, Thinking, and Health* (Grand Rapids, MI: Baker, 2013), 74.

10. William Snyder, "The Good, The Bad and the Ugly of Inflammation," Vanderbilt School of Medicine, February 10, 2015, https://medschool.vanderbilt.edu/vanderbilt-medicine/the-good-the-bad-and-the-ugly-of-inflammation/.

## PRINCIPLE #4: EMBRACE YOUR NO-LOSE SITUATION

1. Gerald F. Hawthorne, *Philippians, Word Biblical Commentary*, vol. 43 (Waco, TX: Word Books, 1983), 39.

2. Warren W. Wiersbe, *Be Joyful: Even When Things Go Wrong, You Can Have Joy* (Wheaton, IL: Victor Books, 1989), 45.

3. Hawthorne, *Philippians*, 45.

4. Hawthorne, *Philippians*.

5. Gerald F. Hawthorne, Ralph R. Martin, and Daniel G. Reid, *The Dictionary of Paul and His Letters* (Westmont, IL: IVP Academics, 1993), 512.

6. Hawthorne, *Philippians*, 18.

7. "The True Death Toll of Covid 19: Estimating Global Excess Mortality," World Health Organization, accessed January 12, 2024, https://www.who.int/data/stories/the-true-death-toll-of-covid-19-estimating-global-excess-mortality.

8. Acts 17:34.

9. Rodney Stark, *The Rise of Christianity: How the Obscure, Marginal Jesus Movement Became the Dominant Religious Force in the Western World in a Few Centuries* (San Francisco: Harper San Francisco, 1997), 83.

10. Stark, *The Rise of Christianity*, 82.

11. Stark, *The Rise of Christianity*, 89.

12. Jeremy Sutton, "16 Decatastrophizing Tools, Worksheets, and Role-Plays," Positive Psychology, September 24, 2020, https://positive psychology.com/decatastrophizing-worksheets/.

13. 1 Corinthians 15:55; Psalm 23:4.

## PRINCIPLE #5: TAKE THE HIGH ROAD WITHOUT FEAR

1. Anonymous, "This World Is Not My Home," first published in 1919, https://hymnary.org/text/this_world_is_not_my_home_im_just _a?extended=true.

2. Bill Gaultiere, " 'Fear Not!' 365 Days a Year," Soul Shepherding, Inc., https://www.soulshepherding.org/fear-not-365-days-a-year/.

3. "Amygdala," Cleveland Clinic, last reviewed April 11, 2023, https://my.clevelandclinic.org/health/body/24894-amygdala.

4. Shawn Achor, The Happiness Advantage: How a Positive Brain Fuels Success in Work and Life (New York: Currency, 2010), 109.

5. Colm Wilkinson, "The Bishop," released 2012, adapted from Les Misérables, by Victor Hugo, https://www.google.com/search?q=the +bishop+lyrics&rlz=1C5CHFA_enUS940US941&oq.

## PART 2: JOY DESPITE PEOPLE

1. Kathleen Kovner Kline, ed., Hardwired to Connect: The New Scientific Case for Authoritative Communities (New York: Broadway Publications, 2003).

2. Kline, Hardwired to Connect, 16.

3. R. F. Baumeister and M. R. Leary, "The Need to Belong: Desire for Interpersonal Attachments as a Fundamental Human Motivation," Psychological Bulletin 117, no. 3: 497–529.

4. Lawrence O. Richards, Expository Dictionary of Bible Words (Grand Rapids, MI: Zondervan, 1985), 480.

## PRINCIPLE #6: GET ON THE SAME PAGE WITH YOUR COMMUNITY

1. Desiderius Erasmus, "Desiderius Erasmus Quotes," BrainyQuote.com, BrainyMedia Inc., 2023, https://www.brainyquote.com/quotes /desiderius_erasmus_110331.

2. Charles Schulz, *Peanuts*, November 12, 1959, Peanuts Wiki, https://peanuts.fandom.com/wiki/November_1959_comic_strips.

3. F. F. Bruce, *Philippians: New International Biblical Commentary* (Peabody, MA: Hendrickson Publishers, 1989), 62.

4. Jim Wilder and Michael Hendricks, *The Other Half of Church: Christian Community, Brain Science, and Overcoming Spiritual Stagnation* (Chicago, IL: Moody Publishers, 2020), 64.

5. Daniel Amen, *You, Happier: The 7 Neuroscience Secrets of Feeling Good Based on Your Brain Type* (Carol Stream, IL: Tyndale, 2022), 245.

6. Amen, *You, Happier*, 256.

## PRINCIPLE #7: ELEVATE OTHERS ABOVE YOURSELF

1. Gerald F. Hawthorne, *Philippians*, *Word Biblical Commentary*, Volume 43 (Waco, TX: Word Books, 1983), 68.

2. Hawthorne, *Philippians*, 69.

3. C. S. Lewis, *Mere Christianity* (New York: HarperCollins, 2009), chapter entitled "The Great Sin."

4. John F. Walvoord, *Philippians: Triumph in Christ* (Chicago, IL: Moody Press, 1971), 51.

5. "Parking Behavior May Reflect Economic Drive," NPR, August 8, 2014, https://www.npr.org/2014/08/27/343623220/parking-behavior-may-reflect-economic-drive.

## PRINCIPLE #8: STOP BEING A GRUMP

1. John F. Walvoord, *Philippians: Triumph in Christ* (Chicago, IL: Moody Press, 1971), 102.

2. Caroline Leaf, *Switch On Your Brain: The Key to Peak Happiness, Thinking, and Health* (Grand Rapids: Baker, 2013), 71.

3. Leaf, *Switch On Your Brain*, 74.

4. Chana Weisberg, "How a Quarter of a Second Can Change Your Life" Chabad.org, January 3, 2010, https://www.chabad.org/blogs/blog_cdo/aid/1073760/jewish/How-a-Quarter-of-a-Second-Can-Change-Your-Life.htm.

## PRINCIPLE #9: CELEBRATE OTHER PEOPLE'S SUCCESS

1. F. F. Bruce, *Philippians: New International Biblical Commentary* (Peabody, MA: Hendrickson Publishers, 1989), 94.
2. Shawn Achor, *The Happiness Advantage: How a Positive Brain Fuels Success in Work and Life* (New York: Currency, 2010), 191.
3. S. L. Gable, G. C. Gonzaga, and A. Strachman, "Will You Be There for Me When Things Go Right? Supportive Responses to Positive Event Disclosures," *Journal of Personality and Social Psychology* 91 , no. 5 (November 2006): 904–17, https://doi.org/10.1037/0022-3514.91.5.904.
4. Bob Buford, https://exponential.org/event/pursuing-next-with-leadership-network/.
5. Jennifer Parr, "Bob Buford's Top Ten Values," Halftime Institute, September 22, 2020, https://halftimeinstitute.org/2020/09/22/bob-bufords-top-ten-values-the-fruit-of-our-work/.
6. Randy Frazee, *The Christian Life Profile Assessment Workbook Updated Edition: Developing Your Personal Plan to Think, Act, and Be Like Jesus* (Grand Rapids, MI: Zondervan, 2015).
7. "Tribute to Dr. Larry Crabb," Hope for the Heart, March 4, 2021, https://www.hopefortheheart.org/tribute-to-dr-larry-crabb/.

## PRINCIPLE #10: DO RIGHT BY OTHER PEOPLE

1. "What to Know About Homesickness and Mental Health," WebMD, reviewed October 25, 2021, https://www.webmd.com/mental-health/what-to-know-about-homesickness-and-mental-health.
2. Gerald F. Hawthorne, *Philippians, Word Biblical Commentary*, vol. 43 (Waco, TX: Word Books, 1983), 117.
3. Hawthorne, *Philippians*, 120.
4. "Do Things for Others," Action for Happiness, accessed January 12, 2024, https://actionforhappiness.org/10-keys-to-happier-living/do-things-for-others.
5. I talk about this experience extensively in my book *His Mighty Strength* (Nashville, TN: Thomas Nelson, 2021).
6. John Bunyan, *Pilgrim's Progress* (London: Wordsworth Editions, 1996).

## PART 3: JOY DESPITE YOUR PAST

1. Steven F. Maier and Martin E. P. Seligman, "Learned Helplessness: Theory and Evidence," *Journal of Experimental Psychology* 105, no. (1976) 1, 3–46, https://doi.org/10.1037/0096-3445.105.1.3.
2. "Our Three Brains: The Reptilian Brain," Interaction Design Foundation IxDF, January 2, 2021, https://www.interaction-design.org/literature/article/our-three-brains-the-reptilian-brain.

## PRINCIPLE #11: STAY CLEAR OF LEGALISM

1. Gerald F. Hawthorne, Ralph R. Martin, and Daniel G. Reid, *The Dictionary of Paul and His Letters* (Westmont, IL: IVP Academics, 1993), 511.
2. *Oxford Language,* s.v. "legalism," accessed January 12, 2024, https://www.google.com/search?q=what+does+legalism+mean&oq=what+does+legalism+mean.
3. Wikipedia; s.v. "*Tetris* effect," last modified September 15, 2023, https://en.wikipedia.org/wiki/Tetris_effect.
4. Shawn Achor, *The Happiness Advantage: How a Positive Brain Fuels Success in Work and Life* (New York: Currency, 2010), 91.
5. Achor, *The Happiness Advantage*, 92.
6. William W. Eaton, et al., "Occupations and the Prevalence of Major Depressive Disorder," *Journal of Occupational Medicine* 32, no. 11 (November 1990): 1079–87, https://doi.org/10.1097/00043764-199011000-00006.

## PRINCIPLE #12: RECALCULATE WHAT REALLY MATTERS

1. John F. Walvoord, *Philippians: Triumph in Christ* (Chicago: Moody Press, 1971), 86. Walvoord mentions these four Greek words for knowledge: *oida, epistomai, suniemi, gnosis.*
2. Gerald F. Hawthorne, *Philippians, Word Biblical Commentary*, vol. 43 (Waco, TX: Word Books, 1983), 138.
3. Kevin Halloran, "Jim Elliot's Journal Entry with 'He Is No Fool...' Quote," Anchored in Christ, October 28, 2013, https://www.kevinhalloran.net/jim-elliot-quote-he-is-no-fool/.

4. Jim Wilder, *Renovated: God, Dallas Willard and the Church That Transforms* (Colorado Springs: NavPress, 2020), 6.

5. The Internet Movie Database; IMDb's page for Harold Abraham quotes from *Chariots of Fire* (1981), https://www.imdb.com/title /tt0082158/characters/nm0002027.

6. The Internet Movie Database; IMDb's page for Eric Liddell quotes from *Chariots of Fire* (1981), https://www.imdb.com/title/tt0082158 /characters/nm0153182.

## PRINCIPLE #13: PUT THE PAST BEHIND YOU

1. Gerald F. Hawthorne, *Philippians, Word Biblical Commentary*, vol. 43 (Waco: Word Books, 1983), 151.

2. Hawthorne, *Philippians*, 105.

3. Olga Khazan, "Running Faster by Focusing on the Finish Line," *Atlantic*, January 20, 2015, https://www.theatlantic.com/health/archive /2015/01/running-faster-by-focusing-on-the-finish-line/384653/.

4. Dan Baker, *What Happy People Know: How the New Science of Happiness Can Change Your Life for the Better* (New York: St. Martin's Essentials, 2003), 224.

5. *Merriam-Webster*, s.v. "plasticity," accessed December 13, 2023, https://www.merriam-webster.com/dictionary/plasticity.

6. Caroline Leaf, *Switch On Your Brain: The Key to Peak Happiness, Thinking, and Health* (Grand Rapids: Baker, 2013), 24.

7. "What Is Epigenetics," Centers for Disease Control and Prevention, eviewed August 15, 2022, https://www.cdc.gov/genomics/disease /epigenetics.htm.

8. "'There Is No Failure in Sports'—Giannis Addresses Comments on 'Failure'," YouTube video, 2:04, during a postgame interview, 2023, https://youtu.be/Xj4icUkwP2A.

9. Daniel Amen, *You, Happier: The 7 Neuroscience Secrets of Feeling Good Based on Your Brain Type* (Carol Stream, IL: Tyndale, 2022), 258.

## PRINCIPLE #14: FOCUS ON THE FUTURE

1. Gerald F. Hawthorne, *Philippians, Word Biblical Commentary*, vol. 43 (Waco, TX: Word Books, 1983), 153.

2. "A Conversation So Intense It Might Transcend Time and Space | John Vervaeke | EP 321," YouTube video, 2:00:39, a conversation between Jordan Peterson and John Vervaeke, January 9, 2923, https://youtube /IZ-tHaHfB8A?si=ULqTHM5XagyGeJ_o.

3. Olga Khazan, "Running Faster by Focusing on the Finish Line," *The Atlantic*, January 20, 2015, https://www.theatlantic.com/health/archive /2015/01/running-faster-by-focusing-on-the-finish-line/384653/.

## PRINCIPLE #15: SURROUND YOURSELF WITH THE RIGHT PEOPLE

1. John F. Walvoord, *Philippians: Triumph in Christ* (Chicago: Moody Press, 1981), 99.

2. Gerald F. Hawthorne, *Philippians, Word Biblical Commentary*, vol. 43 (Waco, TX: Word Books, 1983), 166.

3. Hawthorne, *Philippians*, 166.

4. Karen E. Gerdes and Elizabeth A. Segal, "A Social Work Model of Empathy," *Advances in Social Work* 10, no. 2 (Fall 2009): 114-27, https://doi.org/10.18060/235.

## PART 4: JOY THAT DEFEATS WORRY

1. Linda Searing, "60 Percent of U.S. Adults Are Feeling Daily Stress and Worry, New Gallup Poll Shows," *Washington Post*, April 20, 2020, https://www.washingtonpost.com/health/60-percent-of-us-adults-are -feeling-daily-stress-and-worry-new-gallup-poll-shows/2020/04/17 /13ce9d8a-7ffd-11ea-a3ee-13e1ae0a3571_story.html.

2. "You're Not Alone: Top Things People Worry Most About," *Psychological Health Care* (blog), August 16, 2016, https://www.psychologicalhealthcare .com.au/blog/youre-not-alone-top-things-people-worry-most-about/.

3. Greg Murray, "Why Do We Wake Around 3am and Dwell on Our Fears and Shortcomings?" The Conversation, October 13, 2021, https://theconversation.com/why-do-we-wake-around-3am-and-dwell -on-our-fears-and-shortcomings-169635.

4. Earl Nightingale, "The Fog of Worry (Only 8% of Worries Are Worth It)," Nightingale Conant Corporation, 2023, https://www.nightingale .com/articles/the-fog-of-worry-only-8-of-worries-are-worth-it/.

## PRINCIPLE #16: SEEK RECONCILIATION IN YOUR RELATIONSHIPS

1. Exodus 32:32; Psalm 69:28; 139:16; Revelation 3:5; 20:12–15; 21:27.
2. Dan Baker, *What Happy People Know: How the New Science of Happiness Can Change Your Life for the Better* (New York: St. Martin's Essentials, 2003), 107.
3. Baker, *What Happy People Know.*
4. Daniel Amen, *You, Happier: The 7 Neuroscience Secrets of Feeling Good Based on Your Brain Type* (Carol Stream, IL: Tyndale, 2022), 244.
5. *The Straight Story*, directed by David Lynch (Los Angeles: Asymmetrical Productions, 1999); see also Internet Movie Database; IMDb's page for *The Straight Story*, https://www.imdb.com/title/tt0166896/.

## PRINCIPLE #17: GIVE WHAT TROUBLES YOU TO GOD

1. *Merriam-Webster*, s.v. "magnanimity," accessed January 13, 2024, https://www.merriam-webster.com/dictionary/magnanimity.
2. Lawrence O. Richards, *Expository Dictionary of Bible Words* (Grand Rapids, MI: Zondervan, 1985), 303.
3. Warren W. Wiersbe, *Be Joyful: Even When Things Go Wrong, You Can Have Joy* (Wheaton, IL: Victor Books, 1989), 125.
4. Wiersbe, *Be Joyful*, 126.
5. Gerald F. Hawthorne, *Philippians, Word Biblical Commentary*, vol. 43 (Waco, TX: Word Books, 1983), 183.
6. Hawthorne, *Philippians.*
7. Hawthorne, *Philippians*, 184.
8. C. S. Lewis Quotes, Goodreads, accessed December 13, 2023, https://www.goodreads.com/quotes/1005539-i-pray-because-i-can-t-help-myself-i-pray-because. This is a quote from the movie *Shadowlands*.
9. Dan Baker, *What Happy People Know: How the New Science of Happiness Can Change Your Life for the Better* (New York: St. Martin's Essentials, 2003), 81.
10. "The Science of Thought," JOY!, accessed January 13, 2024, https://joymag.co.za/article/the-science-of-thought/.
11. Daniel Amen, *You, Happier: The 7 Neuroscience Secrets of Feeling Good Based on Your Brain Type* (Carol Stream, IL: Tyndale, 2022), 215.
12. Amen, *You, Happier*, 215.

## PRINCIPLE #18: REHEARSE YOUR BLESSINGS DAILY

1. Deborah Danner, David Snowdon, and Wallace Friesen, "Positive Emotions in Early Life and Longevity: Findings from the Nun Study," *Journal of Personality and Social Psychology* 80, no. 5 (May 2001): 804–813, https://doi.org/10.1037/0022-3514.80.5.804.

2. Shawn Achor, *The Happiness Advantage: How a Positive Brain Fuels Success in Work and Life* (New York: Currency, 2010), 42.

3. Darryl Burton, personal interview with the author, 2023.

4. Miracle of Innocence, https://www.miracleofinnocence.org/.

## PRINCIPLE #19: ACCEPT THAT MORE MONEY AND STUFF ISN'T THE ANSWER

1. Warren W. Wiersbe, *Be Joyful: Even When Things Go Wrong, You Can Have Joy* (Wheaton, IL: Victor Books, 1989), 17.

2. Wiersbe, *Be Joyful*, 198.

3. Gerald F. Hawthorne, *Philippians, Word Biblical Commentary*, vol. 43 (Waco, TX: Word Books, 1983), 200.

4. I covered this topic extensively in my book *His Mighty Strength* (Nashville: Thomas Nelson, 2021).

5. Shawn Achor, *The Happiness Advantage: How a Positive Brain Fuels Success in Work and Life* (New York: Currency, 2010), 210.

6. Dan Baker, *What Happy People Know: How the New Science of Happiness Can Change Your Life for the Better* (New York: St. Martin's Essentials, 2003), 48.

7. *Circulation*, 1994, vol. 89 and https://www.nytimes.com/1994/11/11/us/high-anxiety-raises-risk-of-heart-failure-in-men-study-finds.html.

## PRINCIPLE #20: LET PEOPLE HELP YOU

1. Gerald F. Hawthorne, *Philippians, Word Biblical Commentary*, vol. 43 (Waco, TX: Word Books, 1983), 202.

2. Hawthorne, *Philippians*, 206.

3. F. F. Bruce, *Philippians: New International Biblical Commentary* (Peabody, MA: Hendrickson Publishers, 1989), 154.

4. Warren W. Wiersbe, *Be Joyful: Even When Things Go Wrong, You Can Have Joy* (Wheaton, IL: Victor Books, 1989), 140.

5. Raychelle Cassada Lohmann, "Achieving Happiness by Helping Others," *Psychology Today*, January 29, 2017, https://www.psychologytoday.com /us/blog/teen-angst/201701/achieving-happiness-helping-others.

6. Amy Novotney, "What Happens in Your Brain When You Give a Gift," American Psychological Association, December 9, 2022, https://www .apa.org/topics/mental-health/brain-gift-giving.

7. Novotney, "What Happens in Your Brain."

8. Novotney, "What Happens in Your Brain."

## CONCLUSION: WRAPPING UP THE CHALLENGE

1. "Brain Area Unique to Humans Linked to Cognitive Powers," University of Oxford "News and Events" page, January 28, 2014, https://www.ox.ac .uk/news/2014-01-28-brain-area-unique-humans-linked-cognitive-powers.

# ABOUT THE AUTHOR

Randy Frazee is a pastor at Westside Family Church in Kansas City. A frontrunner and innovator in spiritual formation and biblical community, Randy is the architect of The Story and Believe church engagement campaign. He is also the author of *The Heart of the Story*; *Think, Act, Be Like Jesus*; *What Happens After You Die*; *His Mighty Strength*; *The Connecting Church 2.0*; and *The Christian Life Profile Assessment*. He has been married to his high school sweetheart, Rozanne, for over forty years. They have four children and five grandchildren, with more on the way! To learn more about his work and ministry go to randyfrazee.com.

# You read the book, now live The Joy Challenge.